D0908884

Truck

Previous books by John Jerome

The Sports Illustrated Book of Skiing
The Death of the Automobile

Truck

ON REBUILDING
A WORN-OUT PICKUP,
AND OTHER
POST-TECHNOLOGICAL
ADVENTURES

John Jerome

with drawings by the author

Houghton Mifflin Company Boston

Portions of this book have appeared in *Car and Driver* and the
Vermont *Times*.

Copyright © 1977 by John Jerome

All rights reserved. No part of this work may be reproduced
or transmitted in any form by any means, electronic or
mechanical, including photocopying and recording, or by
any information storage or retrieval system, without
permission in writing from the publisher.

Library of Congress Cataloging in Publication Data

Jerome, John.
On rebuilding a worn-out pickup, and other post-technological
adventures.

1. Motor-trucks—Restoration. I. Title.
TL230.2.J47   629.28'8'3   76-43035
ISBN 0-395-25018-8

Printed in the United States of America

V 10 9 8 7 6 5 4 3 2

There is no Weston, New Hampshire. Strell, Jimmie, and Sepp are still around; Loose Bruce is dead, and we miss him. Marty, my son, isn't thirteen anymore, and still visits from time to time. The Wire King exists, but all of the rest of the people in this book are entirely figments of my imagination. They're not real people at all.

Except for Chris. She is the realest person I know. This book is for her, of course.

Contents

Truck

CHAPTER 1

March

PROBLEM: Hauling horseshit for the garden one barrelful at a time is a depressingly inefficient system.

Solution: Build a truck this summer. The notion is powerful. Add some clear good sense to our grab-bag gardening methods, yes, but that's only the start of it. Think of all the other things we could do with it. Oh, my, yes: a full-time working truck. All of a sudden I can't invent problems fast enough to keep up with the solutions such a truck would represent.

Besides, there's the building of it first, an idea that makes the hair stand up on the back of my neck. Not a whole truck, from scratch, of course — no Truck-Entyre, out of scrap iron and barn junk. Nothing like that. I'll just swap some farmer out of an abandoned pickup truck somewhere in New Hampshire or Vermont, haul the hulk home, take it completely apart, lovingly refurbish and rebuild every single piece of it, and put it back together. I'll end up with supertruck, for next to nothing in investment.

My mind's eye is already romanticizing the process: carefully labeled truck parts all over the barn, tubs of solvent, nuts and bolts in Mason jars, everything sorted by size. Quiet hours of scraping carbon by cozy droplight. New Age hot-rodding, the goals being longevity, use, conservation, rather than more power. Organic hot-rodding? Truck as compost pile?

I should've built my truck in the winter, I think in March — a perfect project for all those days when it gets black dark in midafternoon in northern New Hampshire. Have the whole thing back together and ready to roll for April, when the six-foot drifts start shrinking and some kind of high-center, knobby-tire utility vehicle, basically indestructible, is just right for dealing with the slop of the thaws. But the barn is not heated, not one degree warmer than outside, and the idea of a wrench slipping, cracked knuckles at twenty-four below, is too painful to think about. A while back I grabbed up a hammer and tacks to refasten some peeling exterior insulation and unthinkingly stuck a handful of the tacks in my mouth for handy access. Minus-twenty-degree tacks. Had to come in the house to unfreeze my lips from the chill-steel bastards, took weeks to heal. Besides, I didn't think of the truck thing in time. Winter projects have to be planned ahead up here in the mountains.

Never mind that, it's also a perfect project for summer. Start with the larger picture: resurrection of a truck is hardly ecologically pristine, but at least it is zero-growth in a way, a reclamation of a lot of otherwise condemned and difficult-to-recycle resources. Discarded motor vehicles being one of our society's more unmanageable forms of garbage. Of course the truck, in use, will spew more pollution, but it is pollution that will get spewed one way or another, from some vehicle or other, until we somehow lever ourselves out of this trap of mobility we seem to be in. Until we get the garden producing a hell of a lot more than it seems to want to now.

Small is Beautiful
E. F. Schumacher

It is too easy to get lost in that kind of bogus philosophizing. Maybe the ecological red ink is balanced by the sense of the thing, the gesture. Building a truck will be a rigidly upraised middle finger in the face of the Zoommobiles, the automatic-transmission-with-air-conditioning, fat-lap-of-luxury contemporary National Solution to the problem of transportation. If I can find a truck of just the right age, it'll not only be practical, it'll be a symbolic re-creation of the last rational act on the part of the automobile industry: a private motor vehicle that would actually do work. Instead of slipping over into the soft values, working on the owner's psyche rather than his transportation needs.

Age is important. The basic design of the small utility pickup truck hasn't really changed since about 1939, except for an increase in bed-size. (Now a 4 x 8 sheet of plywood will lie flat in the back. That was the last significant change.) That's why pickups have been such worthy vehicles — with nothing clever done to them since pre–World War II days, they are safely obsolete. Therefore the manufacturers know how to make the pieces that go into them. Know how to make them work.

Unfortunately, trucks are a fad. Pickups and vans, everywhere you look, freaks and surfers and hunters and the resolutely poor, as well as every mechano-constructo-machismo hard-hat who ever yearned to haul a 2 x 4. (Rifle slung across the rear window. *Queasy Rider.*) Chevrolet discovered four or five years ago, to its total confusion, that better than half the small trucks it sold were going for "nontruck uses." A lot of these were pickups for hauling camper bodies (what they call "Okie Boxes" in California). The rest must have gone to soothe the psychological needs of the pseudoagricultural suburbs.

Nontruck use leads to predictable results. You can buy a hard-nosed utility vehicle with nylon-loop carpeting, air conditioning, and factory-installed stereo now. You can spend $6000 on a pickup truck.

Not on mine though. Even if I have to include us among the pseudo-agricultural suburbanites. Chris and I live in Weston, New Hampshire, population 96, about 350 miles from New York City. Some suburb. We are both ex-magazine editors, ex-urban careerists; we moved north in the mid–1960s and still argue over whether we dropped out or dropped in when we did it. We're not really farmers — we periodically go get the cash, through various kinds of free-lance writing and editing, that enables us to live like farmers. I don't think we'll ever go back — the city now makes us very depressed. I'm not too proud of the compromises entailed in this course, or in the acquisition of even the purest of symbolic trucks either. If we were going to go the whole route, I guess we'd have a horse and buggy and haul the manure one shovelful at a time. But we can't yet survive a New Hampshire winter on one horsepower, despite the wonderful things it would do for the compost. Or we don't have the courage to try. So the truck can perhaps be considered a way station on the route to ecological wholeness.

Besides, while I'm at it, I'll look into methane gas converters. There's a man named Harold Bates who is running his car on pigshit over in England right now (proving once again that satire is a dead art). And if there is a problem with methane — we haven't gotten into raising pigs yet — I know I can convert the truck to low-pollution propane.

It is perfectly obvious to *me* why I need a truck. In addition to the horseshit, it will haul the materials in. The materials are the concrete, sand, gravel, lumber, nails, tarpaper, insulation, tools, sheetrock, sewer pipe, furnace and water-pump components, dog food, shingles, paint, and assorted hardware that we seem ever to be hauling to keep our old house and barn erect, ourselves afloat, the operation viable. To get through the winters and . . . to get through the summers. The truck will also haul the other stuff *out*, that being the tag ends of the above, the wastage, oversupply, leftovers, crap. The irreducible, unrecyclable, noncompostable other end of surviving in New Hampshire. It should not be as much as it is; we are reducing it; it still threatens to move us out of house and barn.

Also, unavoidably, there will be hauled the friends, kids, beer kegs, inner tubes, canoes, reclaimed furniture, auction loot, picnic stuff, horse-trappings, bicycles, tools, construction materials for other houses; in short, the rest of our lives. It is not *all* hold-up-the-house-and-batten-down-against-winter here. Hell, there are at least a dozen different/ handy things to do with a truck in connection with Fenton Derby's harvesting bee alone. Fenton is reputed to be the largest noncommercial dope grower north of the Mason-Dixon line, and that usually turns out to be the best party of the summer. Not that you'd want to go hauling the produce around in an open pickup.

I have tried to keep this discussion thus far on a practical, if not downright moralistic, plane. But eventually I will have to confess: <u>the real reason for all this is not so much to have a truck as it is to rebuild it.</u> <u>Doing all that greasy work, making order out of mechanical chaos,</u> <u>turning a worn-out hulk into a serviceable vehicle.</u> The *process.* Lordy, how the notion hangs it in me.

I am a child of the mechanical age, on the downslope of forty, accustomed to thinking in terms of technological solutions. Nuts and bolts. I'm not proud of that either; my gut tells me that that is all over now, that I will keep losing the argument. I am adrift between two futures. Future A is all that stuff best characterized as "software," post-McLuhanistic information bits, maximization, systems analysis. Unacceptable. Future B is Luddite, organic revolution, the land religion. I am circling it nervously. But nuts and bolts have no place here either.

What the truck will really be is a . . . hobby. What a quaint word that is, echoing the 1930s in my head. It'll be my model of the Eiffel Tower built out of toothpicks, my six-foot ball of tinfoil: unscrewing and rescrewing nuts and bolts. Disassembling, cleaning, replacing worn parts, painting, reassembling. Housewifery performed on a relic of the machine age (while the house falls down around me). Preservation of an artifact, yes, but an artifact that will work, that will help ease the transition into that nervous New Salvation. Oh, you can really roll off the old rhetoric about such a project.

I have some idea how to do it, the mechanical part. I figure I can figure it out, or what I can't figure out on my own I can cookbook together, with someone else's recipe. Actually, I did something like this once before, restoring a partial mechanical ruin of a sports car. It worked out okay, although I made some expensive mistakes on a much less extensive kind of project. But that was a totally different kind of machine, different goals, another life. Different sensibilities. That time I daydreamed, while I worked, of hot-shot rootin'-tootin' success, flash and jazz, a superracer. That *was* hot-rodding, a case of car obsession. I was pushing at the limits of what was mechanically possible, hungering to be out at the front of automotive technology. I don't want to be out there anymore, God knows. - This time I will be restoring virtue. I recognize in these fantasies the quality of Canadian documentary films: life in the plains provinces, acres plowed, fertile earth, practicality. Truck images. If I don't watch it, I will begin to imagine that building a truck will somehow melt the rock out of our soil; i.e., one dream is about as much bullshit as the other, and who am I to go sneering at cars-for-status when I am catering so hard to my own psychological aches? What kind of perversion is it to be imagining virtuous hard work while hunkered over greasy truck parts? It won't do to proceed with this line of thought.

But I'll do it anyway, I'll do it, he simpered, warming his hands over the tool section in the Sears catalogue. A truck is real, a truck is plain, we're talking about foot-pounds, loads hauled, tons lifted. Back in the city, in March, they are dreaming over travel folders. Chris sits these evenings surrounded by seed catalogues. I fondle pictures of Sears, Roebuck tools. (The Sears catalogue *is* a travel folder — it doesn't tell you a thing about the surliness of the natives.)

While I am confessing, I must also mention that a lot of my friends have trucks, and they would plan this project a lot differently. Their method is the ultimate scrounging operation. They rescue a truck as it wheezes and staggers toward terminal illness, and thereafter perform the absolute minimum needed to postpone — almost minute-by-minute — the final disaster. A fan belt here, a jury-rigged windshield wiper there, quantities of molasses-thick lubricants to quiet the sounds of impending explosion. Cheaping it together: the freak's version of the rawhide-and-baling-wire tradition of the Depression years. I'm trying to avoid that.

Such an approach has much in its favor, not the least of which is a kind of fatalistic confidence. It doesn't let the motor vehicle and its incipient treachery loom too large in one's consciousness. It is even easier now than it was in the thirties — there are so many more hulks in the graveyards for scavenging. It is also philosophically respectable, by comparison with my own proposed project. My notion involves the absolute foolishness of trying to banish the risks, unavoidable delays, and hard tasks accomplished in miserable circumstances incumbent in the cheap way of keeping the beast in motion. Pissing in the wind, as they say in Texas. Because as any fool can plainly see, those risks, etc., are going to gather themselves about the most religiously restored vehicle, no matter what I do.

I haven't got the nerves for it, however. Waiting until something breaks before I fix it is fine for screen-door latches and light bulbs, but when it involves 3500-pound mechanical devices capable of high rates of speed, such a procedure scares me. Worse, such a method is doomed, these days, to remain resolutely illegal. Safety inspections, licensing requirements, the local cops, all require a certain amount of mechanical forethought that is inimical to the cheap way. Illegal transportation is a sure bet to draw legal attention, and some of my friends can't easily stand legal attention being paid to the private details of their lives. I'm not too fond of it myself.

Much as I admire the spirit behind the run-it-into-the-ground school of vehicle ownership and operation, there is one further disqualification as far as my own plans are concerned. There is no *project* to it. (Or rather, every trip, every use, is a short-term project, which seems to me too scattering of energies.) I also admire projectlessness, but it just won't work for us, for now. It is mid-March already; the geese are due back overhead any day. I doubt if I can explain the psychic lift of that first distant *honk* in the spring, when the passage of the geese seems roughly akin to the arrival of the cavalry just as the Indians are foreclosing on the wagon train. (In the fall, of course, it's another matter.) We once toyed with the idea of throwing a Spring Geese Flight party. A bonfire on the creek bank, a couple of cases of beer, standing there in the snow shuffling from one booted foot to the other waiting for the geese and wishing for Christ's sake the rest of the ice would go out. Abandoned *that* idea quickly enough.

There will be other parties, and I will build a truck this summer over and around them, harvesting bees and all the rest. We are all more than mad this time of year, and I propose, somewhat self-consciously, to launch my search for the perfect (ruined) truck at precisely 7:22 A.M. on

March 20, geese or no geese. The exact moment when the balance is tipped, light against the darkness: spring. Out in Arizona the last straggling remnants of the Hopi will be scattering cornmeal to the east to celebrate the victory of the Sun God over the powers of darkness that have been eating Him away for all these many months. Back home I might just have a ceremonial smoke of my own. With all due respect to the sun. And then set out from the mildly fetid house where we've hung on against the winter, issue forth bravely to find the truck. Giggling.

Ah, what a truck it will be, if not quite rock-bound and copper-bottomed in the New Hampshire tradition, then at least a lean and fat-free New Englander of a truck, long-legged against the frost heaves, hell for stout. When did ever so romantic a notion offer such prospects for eventual utility? The pared-down essence of Yankee ingenuity; such a truck as Ford nor Chevrolet ever dreamed possible. Find it, haul it home, scatter it, fix it, get it back together, yes. Use it up, wear it out, make it do, or do without. A Thoreau's cabin of a truck. Mortised and tenoned together with a little help from my friends. Supertruck. It may not sound like much of an idea, but let me tell you, dreaming over these possibilities got me through one more New Hampshire winter. That's something, right there.

a cut for insertion

tenon

mortise

CHAPTER 2

April

FORGET APRIL. Also May and June, not to mention most of July. In fact, disregard about two thirds of the New Hampshire summer, when all that honest-workingman romance disintegrated into the nervous fidgets. I didn't trip out the door on the vernal equinox as planned; instead we watched New Hampshire settle into mud-month, slit-your-wrists time, when the snow is gone, the sky droops to about a seventy-five-foot ceiling, the thermometer sticks at a steadfast thirty-five degrees, day and night, and the world is endless gray muck, a miasma of not-quite-rain. Day after stinking, bloody day. Firewood and whiskey consumption shoot off one end of the scale, domestic tranquility off the other. It is discover-new-roof-leaks time. It is watch-the-furnace-expire, wreck-the-car, sick-dog, falling-cake, stopped-up-plumbing time.

It is bearable with the sure knowledge that one day the sun will shine again, except that that summer it never did. Watch the garden die: a hard frost on June 10, another on August 4, and then a machine-gun series in the first three weeks of September. Having one's garden wiped out may seem like a personal insult, but it shouldn't irrevocably tangle one's life. Somehow that summer did, and what happened to the garden was eloquently symbolic. Every time we tried to get our shit together, we found ourselves wondering, as the graffiti says, if it's together, what is that other stuff all around it? Which is why, without going into tedious detail, I found myself initiating the search for the truck in late July, totally immune to all that nice ceremony I kept draping around The Plan during the snug-harbor days of late winter.

I looked at a couple of hundred junked trucks in July. I made it to the coast of Maine (a particularly tasty 1940 Ford that turned out to be a wild goose) and nearly to the New York border, didn't quite get into Canada (import duties on junk auto parts?), learned to spot a rusting hulk in my rearview mirror at sixty mph and judge whether or not it was worth the U-turn to check it out. No skill involved, or even a coherent plan; behind the outbuildings of virtually every New England farm there are from three to five mechanical derelicts, just sitting there, no longer even worrying the owner with the lost investment they represent. The worse the farm looks, the better the chances, since the spruced-up and successful places either have their junkers hauled away, or at least push them over a knoll well out of sight from house and road.

The derelicts in question range from flat-beds and dump trucks all the way to tractors, but a high percentage of them are standard farm pickups no longer capable of being maintained in useful condition. Particularly on the economy of a dying family-farm, which is what most New England agricultural relics are. Derelicts doesn't say it by half: beat-to-shit would be a better description. Note: they are not traded in for better machines. They are driven right into the ground, letting out a last dying gasp in the barnyard, immune forever to one more desperate temporary fix that would give another wheezing twenty miles. Dead in the barnyard, pushed behind the nearest building, forever thereafter ignored, unless some sucker comes along. One way you can spot them so quickly is by the patch of weeds. If it's a running truck, you'll see daylight underneath; if it's dead, you have to bushwhack to take a closer look.

The dead vehicles are not traded in on newer models because of the rust. The rust is because of the salt, dumped on the roads all winter to melt the snow. Salt accelerates the oxidation rate of metal. The road salt makes a mushy, corrosive paste that is flung universally about the under- and over-sides of every vehicle. It fouls all the metal parts, pits windshields, scours paint, reduces the useful life of north-country motor vehicles by several years. It also kills roadside trees, pollutes streams and wells, and destroys gardens. It is unnecessary. A coating of unsalted, hard-packed snow is just about as safe (and nearly as fast) as the undependable semifrozen slush that salt makes. But the highway department's goal is bone dryness. No matter how much winter comes dumping down out of the sky. Salt-spreading is the highwayman's fetish; the salt-spreaders work night and day.

(Salt is an invisible tax. We pay for the salt, pay for the machinery to spread it, pay for the labor to get it onto the roads. And then we pay with our vehicles, in reduced resale value, in hulled-out, rotten, disintegrating cars, untimely mechanical failures, a huge additional tax. Salt damage reduces resale value by about $350 a year. Nobody bitches much except the environmentalists.)

Salt damage was the ubiquitous permanent damper on the joys of the truck hunt. Repeatedly, I would find The Perfect Truck and then discover I could poke a finger through the fender. The external damage is the resale-killer, the unsightly cancer that eats away one's financial equity in the machine, but it is superficial. Underneath is where the fatal destruction takes place. Rust melts bolt threads so they simply snap when you try to remove them. Corrosion makes noodle soup out of the spaghetti of electrical wiring, draining the sense out of the neatly ordered linearity of the circuitry. Rust even eats frames: a sufficiently rust-damaged car can virtually break in half.

And I don't weld, don't want to have to learn all that, invest in that equipment. Theoretically you can always add back the metal that is missing, cut out the rotten and tack soundness back in place. Make new, with welding. In practice, "tacking" is the proper descriptive term, and it is only the most skilled who have any kind of success at all. Besides, welding leads to immorality. Short cuts. It is too easy, in the face of the frustrations of dealing with dumb, unyielding steel, to grab a torch and *cut*. What is put back never gets put back quite right, and later falls off again. I wanted no part of the cutting-torch school of automotive mechanics. Besides, welding makes your hair fall out.

What I needed was an Arizona truck, some sturdy wench of a pickup that had spent her adolescence and young adulthood in the high, dry, _{↑RAVEl} salt-free air of the desert. I saw a couple, owned by peregrinating freaks who picked them up on their endless coast-to-coast pendulum swings. (You can't, of course, buy these trucks from the freaks. They are worth too much. See below, Price.) I considered hitching out of snow country, down the road until I stopped seeing salt damage, there to make the first random purchase I thought I could get home with. Logistics defeated that: anything I could hope to drive the thousand or so miles to get back home wouldn't need the care I intended to lavish on it and would be too expensive in the first place. Or I would somehow have to haul it home, which would quadruple the price.

A couple of dozen mildly attractive but ultimately disappointing pickup trucks into my search, I recognized that I was spinning about in what could be, for my original plan, a terminal dither. I didn't yet know what I wanted, or what I planned to do with it, for all those cozy hours dreaming over tool catalogues. It was time to establish some first principles. Age. Make. Degree of restoration. Price. I mean I had to know what I had in mind, didn't I? Or else all that whizzing over the New England countryside was a fun way to spend the summer, but it wasn't going to find me any better equipped for hauling horseshit at the end.

(Oh, but the bubbles that burst on the way. A *perfect* 1950 GMC only twelve miles from home. Not a spot of rust, even the chrome still good. Mr. M. F. Hutchins, about eighty, was tacking new screen to a screen door while we negotiated. Kept tacking away at that screen for four days; every time I dropped by to try to seduce the truck out of his hands, there he'd be, tack-tacking away. He only used the truck to haul around a lawnmower in the summertime, picking up an extra dollar to supplement his social security. Oh God. Mr. Hutchins was obsessed with the care of machinery, telling me to the pint how much oil his 1955 Chevrolet sedan used on its yearly jaunt to Winter Haven, Florida. Oh Christ. I started at $200, went up $50 a day, and at $400 he allowed as how he didn't think he wanted to sell the truck anyway. The canny old bastard had been surveying the market just as busily as I had — that's why he didn't have time to finish that screen — and found out he couldn't replace his jewel at twice the price.)

The '40 Ford on the Maine coast forced me to get my principles straightened out. It was a terribly attractive thing, lean and lithe by modern standards, with a gorgeous old flathead V-8 ripe for loving care. But it cried out for a complete restoration, right down to the rivets in the frame, and it was late July and my panic was rising. Parts would have been impossible, available only through laborious correspondence with the multitudes of old-Ford nuts spread around the country. And even then, they'd bring antique-car prices, which were out of the question.

So prewar trucks were out, better subjects for museum-piece treatment by all those wealthy retirees still worshiping at the shrine of Henry F. My truck had to be, above all else, practical. Postwar Ford or Chevy, not because there is any conceivable reason ever to dispatch another red cent to those two megacorporations, but simply because the two concerns did crank out more pickups than anyone else, and with more of them made, the pickings would be plumper in the junkyards, barnlots, and dustbins where old pickups go to die.

Basically an unsound structure...

Ah, but pre–1960, if possible. Something terrible happened in the 1960–1968 period as far as corrosion protection is concerned, and I was finding 1965 Chevrolet pickups for sale for less money than a decent 1955 model would bring. The pickup truck is an unsound structure. It is a reasonably tight closed box (or globe) of a cab, sitting on the frame rails of a ladder-type chassis. Onto this closed box are attached hood, fenders, doors, none of them capable of bearing any real load, all of them susceptible to rot at the seams. On the back, another box, this one flat and open and totally unbraced in any direction. Once the rust starts (and it always starts), the truck begins to go to pieces rather faster than the more integrated shape of a sedan. With the load-carrying box on the back, for example, it is a race: will the rear fenders pull loose and fall off the sides of the box, or will the forward corners of the box split, and the sides themselves, fenders and all, fall off first?

The "modernization" of pickup styling — in other words, the fiddling around with the shape of the sheet metal — has been in small part to lure customers with something different, and in large part to wrap enough fancy metal around these structural weaknesses to postpone that stage when fenders begin falling off. Rather than increase the gauge of the steel or its resistance to rust, the manufacturers in effect have draped cobwebs of tin over the platonic ideal of the pickup's shape. The fix backfired, of course, resulting in a logarithmic increase in the underside nooks, crannies, pockets, and wells for the salt and snow and ice and crap and corruption to collect in and go to work on the body's soundness. That's what began to happen about 1960.

So okay, a Ford or Chevy between 1946 and 1960. (To be perfectly honest, I really wanted a 1948 Chevrolet, but that was because of an irrational lust from my Texas youth, another country and all that, and I really didn't hope to replicate that juicy relationship.) As for price, $200. Period. That was it, because that is what a truck is worth. Or rather, a truck is worth from about $1000 up if there's little rust, sound mechanical entrails, the cab is good, it is tight and dry and comfy and capable of a couple of years of lightly maintained hard work. Suffering from essential failure in any of those elements, though, a truck is worth $200. Running or not running. I passed up a '65 Chevy, guaranteed inspectable but not, um, at the moment running — for $200. Rust damage. I let a sweet-running '55 go because the bed was so far gone I knew I'd have to replace it entirely, and despaired of finding a repairable replacement up here in rust country. For $200.

I paid $200 for a 1950 Dodge, capable of a creaky and absolutely tentative motion under its own power. Bought it from a freak. I didn't want to do that, stayed away from the communes where I figured any _— not_ useful truck was essential to survival — a loss, if sold, incommensurate _proportion-_ with the $200 gain. But I found a freak who needed $200 to get to _ate_ warmer climes, with a truck that wouldn't get him there.

I didn't particularly want a Dodge, but what the hell, anything I ended up with would have problems, a Dodge no worse nor better than anything else. I tracked a rumor to a commune, to the freak's backyard. Picked my way through kids, chickens, and goats to get a good look at this squat, bull-nosed, blue (cab) and black (bed) half-ton pickup sitting cheerfully at road's end. No weeds under it.

I have to admit that thus far in my search I had been putting some psychic dependence on vibes, hoping that some truck somewhere would speak to me out of the dark well of the mutuality of our fates. Well, maybe not quite like that, but I did expect finally to see a truck and say with certainty that that was the one.

I also have to admit that vibes failed me. There is something too rational in my forty-year-old (used) head, and I kept applying judgments, I suppose. Screwing up the magic. Anyway, nothing emanated, as I stalked the Dodge in its clearing. I poked, prodded, pried, lifted lids, swung doors, climbed over and under. It was all there, mostly sound. A couple of rust holes in the front fenders and running boards (running boards!). The bed was almost solid, the rear fenders eminently suitable for discard. But no vibes, no vapors. I come too late to the nonverbal universe, a word-cat doomed to explicitness. I needed The Word.

I got it, when I heard from the owner. He came out and stood on the verandah of his collapsing farmhouse, barefooted, all wisps of beard and tattered overall galluses, and watched me make three or four circumnavigations of the Dodge before he spoke. Then he gave me The Word:

("This," he actually said, "is your basic truck.")

This is your basic truck

CHAPTER 3

Summer

WAIT, WAIT, this is all wrong. The truck was supposed to be a larky self-indulgence, a nuts-and-bolts playtoy that would lead to a useful tool; there is no real reason for it to lead to this dithering, is there? I am waking in the middle of the night to worry over how to get baby a new pair of brake shoes. The summer is not *all* like that.

I am not, like some I know, a religious skinny-dipper, but I do try to get down to the creek most days. Air my parts, immerse the body, escape the bugs. I guess we always rush the season; last April we were grubbing an asparagus trench while there was still ice in the ground: scrape off four inches, wait a day for the newly exposed earth to thaw, scrape off four more. (Not knowing then as we do now what damage we were doing to the soil quality, how patience would have paid.) I was into the creek in mid-May — Chris claims to have a lower threshold of cardiac arrest — and, I suppose, pushing for New Hampshire to be Arizona by June.

The psychology is all wrong, and that may explain why New Englanders are such cranky bastards. We get what seems like at least six months of the wet, cold, rotten part of spring, the decidedly unbeautiful part, raw and aching. Then we get maybe ten days of soft weather, and pow, everything is three feet high and threatening to strangle us in greenery. That ten days is the crucial time, to get your head straight, slough off the winter metabolism and prepare for the organic explosion to come. (Explosion is the proper term. A ninety-day growing season is a long one — last summer we got only fifty-six days between killing frosts — and yet New Hampshire is as green as anyplace.)

It is possible to get a fat, bright, warm, golden ten days. I seem to recall one year when I put clothes on during that period only to fetch a package personally delivered by the mailman. During these golden spells, the back lanes will be spotted with work crews who have pulled their trucks over to the side of the road, draped themselves over the fenders, and turned their faces up to the sun to bake. Popping six-packs. It is a good time to buy land: everyone is a little sappy.

Last spring it rained the whole ten days.

The reason the ten-day period is so important is that it is followed, soon enough, by the black flies. Or rather the midges, no-see-ums, mosquitoes, deer flies, horse flies, moose flies, and black flies. Nobody takes any clothes *off* when the bugs are biting. If you are quick, ready, on your toes, you get the garden in before the bugs get bad and find pressing indoor matters to deal with until the three- or four-week siege of the bugs is over. The locals always say the bugs only last about a month. I was swatting mosquitoes in the barn in November, after thirty days of killing frost. (Yes, I know it is bad for my karma.) But the bugs are only *bad* — bad enough to drive moose bellowing out of the woods and crashing into the sides of passing cars — for about a month.

No, wait, that's all wrong too. Frost, mud, bugs. It isn't necessarily that way, it is only a point of view when things are stacking up. New Hampshire is where we live on purpose, difficult as that may be to reconcile with the foregoing. I never said there weren't itchy periods.

It's the itch that makes us jump the season on the asparagus trenches. The snow has been gone for three or four weeks, and every day the sun spends a little longer toying with the garden patch. Every windowsill in the house is full of seedlings, too early to put any of them out yet, but the house is filling with the damp-earth smell from watered pots. Becoming a greenhouse, the smell and the humidity making chemical changes in the blood of the inhabitants. A guaranteed scientific fact. Too early to *do* anything, though, and we can barely stand it.

Finally it is just too much, and we giggle about the house putting on too many clothes, mud boots and ragged sweaters, and get out. Clang around in the corners of the barn, dragging out shovels and forks. Nice, robust noises from the falling garden tools; raw spring wind airing out the barn. We pick the spot, scraping ineffectually at first, relearning how to work with muscles that haven't done anything but haul firewood since December. Get into the rhythm of it, slicing through loamy mud down to the ice, laying back a row, exposing the hard heart of the winter's frost. Spots of sun race by; Jesus, it feels fine the first time you get a few minutes of hard sun on your back, and start shedding sweaters. Entertaining mystic notions of how, if it does that to your back, it must be passing *miracles* in the soil.

We end up on hands and knees, gloves shed, hands raw and red but finally accustomed to the cold, grubbing away with skinned fingers down to the frozen brown ice-mud, wet to the knees. Noses running, backs aching. Stay at it too long, collecting the aches, until we can't stand *that* any longer either and finally quit. Survey the glop we have made for a minute — here's where the asparagus will go, two more years until we get to eat it — and then almost run, staggering, to the house, to strip, sluice off the mud with hot water, soak, rub some kind of fragrant grease — Corn Huskers Lotion (trademark registered) is good — into the ravaged knuckles. Steaming tea, or maybe a little bourbon, while we sit around on the backs of our necks, talking about our glorious aches in the unaccustomed later light of spring evening. Too warm from the tub and tea to sit in the house; maybe a stroll outside to blow the fine, distillate, postbath sweat off. Feel how, yes, sure enough, the wind is still sharp. A few more weeks. Tomorrow, another four inches.

Or later, when it's almost summer, when we go into the creek for the first time of the year. What we do is, we wait for a hot day when we are doing really rotten work. Clearing brush, shoveling shit, something really awful. We realize that maybe it *is* hot enough, maybe it has been warm long enough, an idea we toy with while we grunt away at what we're doing. We find we have picked up the pace, are going at it like killing snakes: I mean we are really working at getting *hot*, pouring sweat. Then just before we faint, we take off at a dead run, galloping down the steamy, shady path through the alders, kicking off shoes and tearing at our clothes as we go.

It doesn't matter how hot we were or how fast we ran to get there, by the time we are bare-assed on the rocks at the creek bank we are cold again. The rocks, Christ, they're still practically pure ice, and we dance about in bare feet, thinking we'll wait until the sun gets really hot again, thinking that no matter how warm the days get, it is still dropping to about forty degrees every night to rechill the creek. And to go into that water isn't a pause to refresh oneself on a hot day, it is a goddamn *dare*.

But maybe it won't be so bad — and I usually slip and fall in about that point anyway. It is worse than I believed possible. I experience total pain. I am struck rigid, barely able to summon the coordination to scramble out. I explode out of the water, scratching for purchase on the slippery rocks. Out. I stand immobile, muscles locked from jaw to toes, dying. Waiting for the pain to fade.

It does; the glow starts. I can almost hear the blood hum as it seeps back up near the surface of my skin. I saunter up the path collecting the sweaty rags I shucked as I plunged down to the creek, strolling naked to the house with a handful of clothes. Prickly path on still tender feet, summer air drying the water on my ass, skin beginning to turn pink, my body a blast furnace overcompensating for the shock. I get to the house, dry off, slip on something thin and soft. Pad about the cool kitchen linoleum barefoot, newly opened windows and doors swirling the house full of bee sounds and hot growing odors. Still glowing. Damp hair on the back of the neck. Still glowing. Oh, there is a mellow electric humming in the world on an early summer New Hampshire day. And it is going to be summer all summer long.

None of that has anything to do with truck selection or rebuilding, of course; it is more like survival tactics. It is necessary from time to time to shift the perceptions 180 degrees, look from the top down instead of the bottom up. No, that's too easy. It is more like picking one's times, knowing when to lie low. The official state tree of New Hampshire is not the tamarack, but it should be. The tamarack is basically a worthless tree for purposes of shade, firewood, or lumber. It inhabits a curious borderline between the deciduous and the evergreens, having cones and firlike needles that fall off in the wintertime. In the summer, it is a wispy pest, attracting insects and weeping sap. In the winter it is only one more straggly gray figure on the horizon.

But it grows tall, arrow-shaped, and in the spring it fuzzes out early with a sharp green jolt, a light haze of color coming into focus against the dead gray of the expiring winter. First sign that the siege is over. And in the fall, after the conventional show from the maples, the tamarack hangs on after the woods have gone back to gray. Then it turns a brilliant, fiery yellow, vertical golden stripes up on the hillsides. For a couple of weeks, it is glorious. We have one in the back, and in early November it lights up the house reflecting the sun.

That doesn't have anything to do with trucks either. There is no neat moral lesson to the tamarack, but the timing is nice. Over in Maine they call them hackmatacks. I don't know why.

CHAPTER 4

August

MEANWHILE, back in truckland: "I was kind of thinking $225," said Elbow, which is what the owner was calling himself.

What was this? A violation of the existing order? A truck was worth $200, everybody knew that (everybody in the activity of inspecting old pickups, anyway). What was this $225 supposed to represent? I was struck dumb; I made another circuit of the Dodge, trying to figure out what it was I was supposed to say.

My silence evidently made Elbow nervous. "Well," he said, "I just said that so you could offer something else." He smiled sweetly. "And then we could go back and forth. You know."

We settled for $200.

Elbow delivered. There were legal complications resulting from his license plates on my truck, so he managed to get it into motion and in fact to get it all the way to my place, complete with a box of unidentifiable spare parts and the remainder of a dollar's worth of gas. Then I drove him home in the other car while he unloaded the truck's history, faults, liabilities. No point in slippery salesmanship with a $200 truck. It had once been a plumber's friend down south, hence the mildness of the rust damage. Condemned at least once before in its life, for unknown ailments, and then bought out of a junkyard by a friend of Elbow's, who happened to acquire a $100 bill and went looking for transportation. Seventy-five bucks for the truck, and $24.50 for enough other miscellaneous parts to get it running, inspected, and licensed, leaving fifty cents for gas out of the legendary hundred-dollar bill.

The Dodge had had at least one more engine since that time and was currently powered by a '53 replacement with two short rods. The starter motor was rotten, there was a split in the gas tank that limited capacity to a very few gallons at a time, and a steering arm was bent so badly that the truck hunted down the road like a hound trotting sideways, trying to pick up a scent. It would hold a little oil pressure, if I used heavy enough lubricant, and would run almost forty mph if I dared. A fine truck, all things considered. I whizzed Elbow home in an absolutely manic state, in a lather to get back and get my hands finally on my truck.

We had backed it to the door of the barn. We slapped on my own set of illegal license plates. Marty, my thirteen-year-old son from my first marriage, visiting for a couple of weeks, helped me clear enough crap out of the barn so we could put the truck inside and begin work. We put the crap directly onto the truck, built up a reasonable load, and set out on a test run to the town dump. Demonstration number one of the basic goodness of trucks: half an hour of ownership and already it is doing work for us, helping eat through the clutter in the barn to make its own place to stay. Two hundred yards down the road toward the dump, it caught on fire.

Here we are, swaying down the road trailing old screen doors, scrap lumber, and tire casings, while I whipsaw the wheel from one steering lock to the other, trying to find an attitude that will keep us out of the ditches. Smoke begins pouring up through the floorboards, and we are choking on the acrid stink. I have visions of that cracked fuel tank, the degree of slosh that my inexperienced steering has imparted to its contents. Marty, with a quicker brain and a stronger instinct for self-preservation, has a hand on the door handle and feet planted for a dive into the softest available ditch.

The parking brake on those old Dodges was a small drum on the drive shaft, completely separate from the vehicle's road braking system. They never worked, those old drive-shaft parking brakes, but I had set the brake anyway while we loaded the truck. And had forgotten it when we drove off. It let us get up to road speed before it decided to perform its duty, and then began smoldering as it tried to bring us to a shuddering halt. Finally, as I felt the truck begin to labor and sigh under the braking load, I twigged to the source of the problem, hit the brake handle, and presto, we shot forward again. No point in stopping to let the flames lick at the gas tank, about a foot from that smoldering brake lining. I floored it. The wind blew out whatever had caught fire and cleared the smoke from the cab so we could see again. We drove on to the dump, making wry insinuations about each other's cowardice in the face of emergency. Nothing still smoldered by the time we stopped.

And it didn't matter anyway, so long as we didn't go up in smoke. That was the *point:* that last shuddering run to the dump was indeed a test flight, an inventory of the degree of disaster, all to be made new in months to come. Once we were home from the dump, we backed the truck up to the barn again and began groaning away at the solidly rusted bolts that held the bed on the back. Six bolts — two of them snapped, two had to be chiseled, two actually worked like bolts are supposed to — and a few wires, and everything from the cab back could be tipped off onto the ground. The truck came out from under its truckness, its load-carrying capacity stripped away like a shell off a turtle. From working truck to mere self-propelled people-carrier, and an odd-shaped one at that. I unbolted the hood and dropped the exhaust system. Managed to make the

Out from under its truckness

failing starter work one more time, the unmufflered engine rasping like a sick racing car, and backed it into the barn. Shut it off. Hung the key on a nail over the door. Done. Silence. The truck would reemerge, in however many months, all new. A whole new truck.

The next step, according to my careful plan, was slow and methodical disassembly, perfect order, labeling of pieces and planning of the campaign. I had even bought a batch of string-tag labels, virgin white, with which I proposed to enforce order. But I began walking around that tired old Dodge, taking off a piece here and there, examining it, tossing it aside for storage later — when I figured out where everything would go — and I lost control. About the second time I had to stop what I was doing, untangle a label string with greasy fingers, hunt up a pencil, manage to tie the goddamn thing somewhere so it wouldn't fall off and get lost, and painfully letter some bit of invaluable information like "battery" or "fender" on it, I gave up on the procedure as basically fetishist. Later. I would figure out all that stuff later, I kept telling myself.

Elbow was right: the 1950 Dodge *is* your basic truck. When we first moved onto our ten acres, it was autumn. After the cheap-jack Walt Disney display of the foliage change, when the leaves were finally gone and the understory growth withered and turned gray, we suddenly discovered that we could see the shape of the land. We had walked it all before a dozen times, but no clear shapes had emerged from the woodiness; now, between foliage and snow, the bare bones of the terrain became visible and we could see what we had bought. Chris pointed out that the same thing was true of the truck. It was only when the pieces began coming off, the bones showing through, that the basic shape — the simplicity — came into view.

A 1950 Dodge is a square and stocky-looking thing, with an unusually deep bed, simple half-round rear fenders, a two-piece hood that has to be propped open one half at a time, and molded-in, integral front fenders. A

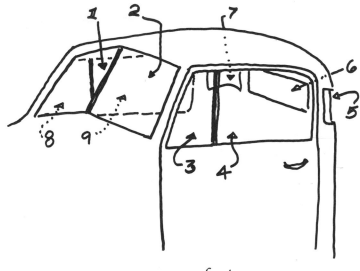

Nine pieces of glass

very boxy cab, with funny little curved rear quarter windows. There's a two-piece windshield, plus wing windows, door glass, the quarter windows, and a rear window, which makes nine separate pieces of glass (without giving all that much visibility). The grille is simply three bars across the front, long gone from mine — which leaves six horizontal slits in the front-end sheet metal, and nothing to rattle. Basic truck. Inside is a wide bench seat (replaced, on my truck, with a racy red-and-white plastic number from a passenger car, and never bolted down, so that it had a tendency to slide from side to side, out of phase with the steering lurches, as the truck meandered down the road) and lots of head and leg room, a three-speed column shift, and a standard complement of miscellaneous other controls, some of which, on my truck, still worked.

Underneath all that deep and broad and boxy, however, was only a slightly magnified Model A Ford, or the 1950s equivalent thereof. Two hefty frame rails, tied together here and there with a cross-member. A beam axle with leaf springs at the front, and a beam axle with leaf springs at the rear. About 900 pounds of archaic, long-stroke, L-head six-cylinder engine slung in between. All of it absolutely straightforward, stolid, devoid — I sincerely hoped — of trickery. The American Automobile, circa 1933, in all its mechanomarvel simplicity. Trucking version. The differences that seventeen years of automotive evolution had made were of dimension and detail: a couple of extra cylinders, better lubrication, improved metallurgy. A little thickening here and there, where twenty years of experience had shown that breakage might occur. Changes only to make what they had work better, last longer, not give out.

As the bones began to show, my luck continued to astound me. I really didn't know what a 1950 Dodge pickup was when I bought it, had acted on hunch and that one-line sales pitch about basic truck. But the deeper I dug into it, the more two things impressed me. In the first place, it was *all right*. Oh, sure, the steering and brakes were shot, the engine had to be rebuilt completely, the wiring was a miracle of hope, blind luck, and low wattage. It needed some work, and in fact I had performed a considerable public service in getting it off the road for a while. But it was all there, and all seemed to be sound or repairable. There was not that fatal, total flaw which would scotch the whole project. In its God-knows-how-many-hundred-thousand miles, it had held.

Which was undoubtedly because of the second impressive realization, also emerging: it demonstrated the thesis. It was a perfect working model of obsolete machinery. It was, by all that dynamic obsolescence holds holy, so *dumb.*

The parent corporation, Chrysler, has been selling itself to the public on the basis of "superior engineering" for decades. An example of that superior engineering: back in the Mesozoic period of automobiles, some Chrysler engineer decided that since the wheels on the left-hand side of the car were turning in a direction that corresponded to the loosening, rather than the tightening, of standard bolt threads, it therefore would be safer to have reverse-thread, or left-handed bolts holding the wheels on the left-hand side of the car. A lot of extra expense and bother, but . . . *engineering.*

In 1970 Chrysler abandoned reverse-thread lug bolts on the left-hand side of its cars and trucks. One of those engineers must have realized, after about fifty years of close observation, that sure enough, none of the wheels were falling off the competition's cars, which had your ordinary, right-hand-thread wheel fastenings. If I seem abnormally concerned with the direction of rotation of the bolts that hold the wheels on Chrysler products, it is because I didn't know, at the outset of this farce, about this Chrysler-product peculiarity. Didn't find it out until I was brought simultaneously to the edge of hernia and despair by the intransigence of those left-side wheel bolts. Here I was, planning the ultimate disassembly operation, and I couldn't even get the bleeding *wheels* off my truck.

Yes, Chrysler Corporation engineering would have to be characterized as conservative even today. And the 1950 Dodge pickup? By comparison a hammer is an exercise in imaginative technological accomplishment.

So, well, after a busted lug bolt or two I did get the wheels off, and a lot more. As a matter of fact, in August, mad vandalism set in. I began to go at the truck like a small boy with a busted alarm clock. Bed and hood stacked outside the barn, to disappear under the winter snows — a winter out of reach of the salt, for once. Onto jack stands with the truck. All the plugs pulled — engine oil, transmission and rear-end fluids, radiator drained. Off with the accessories — air cleaner, carburetor, horn, battery, generator, fuel pump, starter, oil lines, water hoses, wiring, distributor. Radiator out. A stack of blackened, greasy lumps, a pile of necessities growing alongside as the engine gets more and more naked. A jury-rig of chains and tackle over a foot-square beam in the

A lot of creaking and nervousness

barn rafters, a lot of creaking and nervousness as the winch is tightened, a final dive underneath to loosen everything at the back of the engine — bell housing, transmission, clutch, motor mounts — and then the slow, totally scary extraction of the engine. Too goddamn heavy to fool around with: the whole larky notion of truck-as-plaything very suddenly turned into a serious undertaking. And finally this 900-pound boulder of an engine, lying on the floor, trickling the last of its life-fluids out onto the ancient cowshit. And me capering around it like I'd just removed the capstone from the top of the Great Pyramid at Giza.

Of course that took about a month. Should've taken a day, by a mechanic's standards, but there is this problem of competence that has to be considered. I have slid over that so far, in all the manly talk about hammers and nails and such. Wrenches and winches. But I am approaching this project bereft of total competence. I've been thinking about it a lot lately.

There are people who, when they nail up a board, for example, will see clearly the width, length, and strength needed, cut the board to fit, select nails that will not split the wood, drive them firmly into board and backing, and the task will be done. I can envision this, but I am not one of these people. I keep asking myself, why is this? I grew up around a man who was "handy," good with his hands, as they say. None of his skills rubbed off. (In fact I resisted them fervently, which is one answer right there. And, thirty years later, value them perhaps too highly, which is another.) More important, when I was younger it never occurred to me that skills were involved. A kid sees a hammer, and it is obvious that what you do is pick up the thing and pound away with it. A saw you just push back and forth and it cuts things in two, right?

As there are skills to be acquired in the operation of hammer and saw, so are there with wrenches. There is even a frontwards and a backwards to a wrench, despite the fact that obviously, well, I mean look at it, I just put it on the nut and *turn* the bugger, don't I? The backwards wrench will turn the nut as effectively as the frontwards wrench, until the nut becomes hard to turn. Then the backwards wrench slips off, and the wrench-wielder's skin gets pierced.

The frontwards wrench slips off too, under sufficient pressure. All this is only one step up from the self-evident; one quickly learns back from front in wrenches. But one does have to learn. And lying on one's back, particles of ancient road-grit peppering one's eyes, an arm thrust up into the bowels of the machinery to search in the darkness for a nut that may or may not be within reach, one doesn't ponder the fine points of backwardness and frontwardness. One proceeds, in that situation (aching muscles strained to the snapping point, confident of imminent suffocation from the falling debris, hands growing slick from dripping oil and grease) in a kind of fog of mechanical hysteria. Zip. Skinned knuckles.

It is in such situations that reflections on competence occupy the mind. I am not going to clown this up with black comedy about the pints of hot solvent in the face and tangled feet in the droplight extension cord. There was all of that, and some of it almost funny, but I don't think that that is the point. Rather, it is a learning process, and some of it, eventually, I began to learn. An interesting accretion of bits of sureness — the hand up in the mechanical entrails begins to know its way in the dark, picks up the wrench frontwards to start with. It is the beginning of competence. I picked up speed.

(There is an added contradiction in that although I am just learning my way about wrenches, I do know a little about automobile mechanical theory. Paper knowledge, abstract. I know principle but have always escaped practice, and had the arrogance to assume that one took care of the other, despite the hoary cliches about the difference. I was to puncture this arrogance as regularly as I did the skin of my knuckleš.)

It turns out that the practice doesn't have too much to do with wrenches anyway. It deals more regularly with a thousand little tricks that one eventually learns to make metal more manageable. Leverages, cheater bars, taps and knocks. Searches for the pressure point, the key, the hidden spring which is never a spring at all but only a different way of working. Hammers. For years I've heard jokes about the get-a-bigger-hammer school of auto mechanics, usually developing out of military mechanical training. Scornful jokes. A dozen times in the first weeks of disassembly, I would struggle to free some frozen metal part by unscrewing, by prying, finally by tapping gently at first with the wrong tool, then with a carpenter's hammer, a mechanic's ballpeen, and at last, in virtual rage, I would get the ax from the woodpile, turn it blade upward, and go ahead and *hit* the goddamn thing. Pop, and it would be loose, undamaged. The problem was, sometimes I spent days cleaning, searching for a joint, an advantage, tap tap tapping with too small a hammer, too tentatively. And sitting and staring, trying to invent ways of getting at it.

Inevitably, I suckered for a small boy's dream of competence. Initiation rite: if I could rebuild a truck, then I would be, beyond all Freudian worminess, demonstrably an adult. Assuming transliteration of totally unrelated skills, as in my unconscious assumption that ownership of a working truck would make the soil turn fertile. There is a connection here between those times when the fish would not bite and my father would tell me I wasn't holding my mouth right, but I don't think I can pin it down at the moment. Distracted as I am by truck details.

Actually I discovered the size of the problem more clearly with the barn than with the truck. Those March dreams of a summer of truck-building were blown to hell, and the truck was to be a winter project after all. That meant making the barn warm, or truck parts on the kitchen table all winter. Making the barn warm involved, primarily, insulation and working doors, and secondarily, installation of a wood stove, removal of a couple of milking stalls, addition of some lights. The carpentry was a time trip: the 2 x 4s in that barn measure 2 inches by 4 inches, which was startling in itself. (Buy a 2 x 4 today and you get a piece of wood measuring 1½ by 3½ inches, which may also explain what happened to the price of crude oil or something.) Out of the walls came 1898 Boston newspapers, frontier insulation. The last cow had been quartered there in the 1930s, and all the smells had softened to a rich, organic warmth. It was a nice place to work.

However, from time to time my intelligence failed. Whoever built that barn built solid, and I was trying to unbuild in the best New England tradition, every board saved to go someplace else later, nails pulled carefully. Disassembly, rather than demolition. And there were joints I could not unlock, seams I couldn't spring. The carpentry was a Chinese puzzle, the barn a seamless box. I started gently, with a small hammer and lots of patience. I ended up forecasting the future, getting the ax and the wrecking bar and busting things apart. I couldn't dope it out. I was confounded by the cleverness of a turn-of-the-century farmer, who likely only carpentered to pass the time in bad weather, in between spells of real work out in the fields.

Here I was proposing to tackle the mechanical intricacies of the automobile age and I couldn't decipher the hammer-and-nail simplicity of barnyard carpentry. While simultaneously I was trying to tear down a truck, and I'll be honest with you, I wasn't having such good luck with that either. A month to get the engine out. Ridiculous.

There was a moment *before* the engine was out that was worse. It was in early September, just after Labor Day. I was fooling around with the dog at seven-thirty in the morning, relieved that the streams of summer tourists would now be gone, lessening the traffic on the road. Just juking around in the fields, wasting time, watching the dog make a fool of herself over a ruffed grouse. A bit nervous about the significance of the hard coat of frost on the ground cover. Then, overhead, faintly: *honk!* Shit. That's right, ducks. Headed south. A month early. The barn not finished. The hard, iron hand of winter about to slam the door. Darkness and cold and never any end to it, and the engine not even out yet, and I'm not even sure the goddamn beam for the engine hoist will hold. It will break, and drop 900 pounds of dead Dodge engine on me, and there is no way, no way at all it is possible. Not any of it.

CHAPTER 5

Close to Godliness

HIGHS AND LOWS, lows and highs. What I knew in my head but was yet to come to understand in the small of my back was that I really had to clean the bugger up. First. Another truism, like the one about the $200 price: a truck is filthy. There are seven or eight identifiable kinds of filth involved, before one gets to the really challenging stuff.

Some former owner, for example, had spilled a couple of quarts of used engine oil under the seat in the space provided for tool storage. This space does, providentially, drain — particularly on my truck, where the back wall of the cab and the floor had long ago parted company along about three feet of the seam. Drained oil leaves a considerable residue, so somebody had dumped on it about five pounds of the pulverized clay compound used for soaking up oil and grease from garage floors. (Same stuff that is used for commercial Kitty Litter. Maybe the former owner . . . no.) Said cleaning compound changes, upon contact with oil, from tiny clean white pebbles of clay to sticky black pebbles of clay — and then just lies there, holding the oil in place, unless it's swept up. Add a hundred thousand miles or so of cigarette butts, candy wrappers, disintegrating seat upholstery, beer can pop-tops, old ball-point pens, small mechanical parts, road dirt, shoe scrapings, melted crayons, dog hair, turnpike receipts, and a bale of lint. As one begins to tackle such a mass, one begins to suspect that it may well be the glue which holds the truck together. And in fact that mass must be removed, not out of any finicky anal compulsion toward neatness, but in order to discover what's under it, where soundness lies, what has to be fixed. To find out if it is indeed the essential glue.

That was the easy part, the topside — under the seat, wedged into the floorboards, stuffed up under the dash, overflowing the glove box — so to speak. The rest of the truck was covered with a one- to four-inch layer of congealed road tar and gravel, an amalgam which makes a kind of undercoating but which does not, unfortunately, prevent rust. And where the road tar doesn't reach, the leaking seals and gaskets, the loosely assembled engine, the trauma of hard use, had flung a mixture of the various fluids associated with motor vehicles, plus purest dirt. Distillations and settlements of hydraulic fluid, grease, oil, gasoline, gasket cement, paint, battery acid, dirt. Steamed, baked, and burned into place. To be removed, all of it, before anything could sensibly go back into place.

No point in making an epic of this: it was pleasant enough work, once I got used to the idea of getting totally grungy whenever I went near the truck, got used to breathing all the noxious crap that inevitably floated about the process. With the engine out, I pulled off all the rest of the engine bay garbage, disconnected the various cables and levers linking cab and components. Disconnected and removed all the instrumentation and underdash stuff. Pulled out all the wiring in one continuous (rotten) string, in order to send it away for duplication (first step in a long downward slide of misplaced intentions, a tiny little original sin). Dropped the transmission and drive shaft. Looked at my truck and thought, well, now, I'm ready to begin. As soon as I get it cleaned up.

It is automatic to look for symbolic points of departure in such a process, moments when the energy renews itself as the direction of the labor changes. There sat the truck, up on stands. Bare, stripped cab, still joined to the front fenders only because I couldn't bust loose the rusted bolts. Stripped chassis, with no distractions left on it but springs and axles, and what is there to learn about them anyway? Well, yes, there is the differential still in place in the rear axle, and I do have to get into that eventually, and, um, steering, that has to come down, and of course the brakes, backing plates, wheel bearings, axle seals . . .

The trouble with symbolic points of departure is that you never get to them in order to turn around and depart. There were a dozen times when I stepped back, wiped my hands, and said, "There. Now. Time to *begin.*" And then noticed some other assembly that had to come apart to reveal another beyond that. A dozen times I said the hell with it, that's it, the disassembly has to stop somewhere, else I will be going all the way back to stone axes to chop the trees to heat the forge to smelter the steel to assemble the truck that Jack built. Each time I declared a final halt in the disassembly, I then remembered that other seal which would fail if not replaced, the additional point of wear that if left unchecked would surely be the first to let go once I got the truck back together and could no longer get at it without major disassembly again. (A major contributor to my patience was the realization that the truck would never again be so easy to work on as it was scattered about my barn.)

I started cleaning long before I reached that mystical turn-around point. Not too bad. A putty knife, pocketknife, a couple of screwdrivers. Paintbrushes, petroleum-based solvents, a bucket of soapy water — by late fall usually simmering on the wood stove. A couple of wire brushes, and a couple more wire-brush wheels and cups for a quarter-inch drill. A hammer and chisel for the really tough stuff. And an unlimited supply of hours.

Take up a chunk of truck, and make a kind of initial cut, scraping away the topmost layer — a layer that curls away like orange rind, that is anywhere from an eighth of an inch to two inches thick, composed of ropy, self-adhesive, utterly black dreck. Get the edges and the flat surfaces exposed, the actual dimensions of the metal established. Hit it with the wire brush for a while. Daub on some solvent, and go back to the putty knife — mankind will someday realize that the putty knife may be its most useful invention. Wipe, daub, scrape. Repeat. See this carefully designed metal intricacy begin to take shape out of what was a lumpy black mechanical turd. Trace the finer crevices and recesses with pocketknife, furrowing out ribbons and threads of accumulated dead grease. Polish it off with wire brush and quarter-inch drill, sending a fine spray of solvent and dirt over truck, tools, walls, face. Wash it down with soap and water and put it aside for overhaul, or, if there's nothing to fix, a coat of paint. Rust-Oleum, of course, the fish-oil-base primer that is supposed actually to resist rust. Pick up another. Only about 7000 or maybe 2,000,000 parts, roughly, to your basic truck.

It is not a task that challenges the intellect. Wipe, daub, scrape. No particular accretion of competence here. Wipe, daub, scrape. Sometimes the sequence has to be repeated four or five times before any real headway is made against the accumulated gluck. Scrape. It is in fact mindless stone-daze-stunned stupefaction. Gettin' it clean to get it together to take it out and get it dirty again. Let's put the truck loop on, Charlie, everybody likes to dance to that one.

Stoned-out and loopy is the accurate term. I start in cleaning parts with my head straight as the chief of police; I sit there with my hands in the greasy grit, letting them do the thinking, and my head starts going away on me. Far, far away. In twenty minutes I am out of sight, the truck loop blasting away in the deserted concert hall of my vacant head. Some of the most inane interior monologues — or dialogues, or group scenes — since the last Pentagon staff meeting start gibbering away in my skull. No dope necessary: cleaning parts bends my head enough all by itself.

Now, I am not disposed to give names to mechanical devices. Like when a cute girl says about your car, "Oh, it's so cute, what's its name?" and so you think up a cute name for it, the Green Dragoon or Hermione or Toad, something like that. I won't try to argue that there is not a spirit of the machine, that when several hundred standardized pieces — standardized, but necessarily diverse, even if microscopically so — are linked together the way they function can generate a kind of personality. That for all the standardization and assembly-line techniques, one 1974 Ford (or 1950 Dodge truck) may be vastly different from its mechanical duplicate, in affect if not in specification. In personality, if you will (the Lemon Theory, which any child of technocracy will tell you is an impossibility). I can see that. I've just always resisted the additional step, personifying the machine with a name. Cloying.

Nevertheless, a month or more of scraping dirt off pieces of metal sent my head to some weird places and weakened my resistance. There was, for example, a three- or four-day meditation on 1950. What that meant. The truck was built the year I graduated from high school (now my eldest child has finished college). That part of 1950 — my own narrow New Braunfels, Texas, scene — I remembered fairly well, but what was the *world* doing back then? Korea, for Christ's sake, what did that mean? After I got through all the nostalgia junk — penny loafers and rolling up the bottom of my blue jeans — what else was happening?

Truman was President, that feisty little man who looked like my Uncle Looie, looked like everybody. Could he possibly have been the President? Fantasy material for endless hours, right there. If I had the chance, what would I have said to Harry Truman? Other than "Give 'em hell, Mr. President"? This truck, Mr. President, was clanking down the assembly line in Hamtramck, Michigan, even as you were banging out "The Missouri Waltz" on the White House piano. A fitting juxtaposition, Mr. President: both of you products of Middle America, both of you emerging before that epithet came to symbolize all that is stolidly mean, pinched with fear, resolutely joyless in the American people. Sturdy Midwestern stock, the both of you. No-nonsense practicality, never a whiff of the mystical. Dropped the bomb to stop the war, period, slap-dab practical, get it over with. Never confused the issue for a moment with any of that philosophy guff, those wispy Oppenheimers quoting the *Bhagavad-Gita*. No nuclear soul-searching. You got an atom you want split, just split 'er. Put her down right here; get a bigger hammer.

Yes, Mr. President, you were a jaunty little pickup truck of a President, all right. Eisenhower was a dowdy Chevrolet family sedan, Kennedy a sleek Irish Ferrari, Johnson an overblown Lincoln limousine. Nixon was an Edsel, a hollow shell constructed out of motivational research and rigged consensus, rather than metal. But you were metal, yes sir, hard steel, a worker. Throw the tools in the back and hop in, get on to the next job. Haul MacArthur's ass back home, don't take any cheap shit off the generals. Let him huff and puff to the Congress; it don't hurt the runnin' of it none.

Oh, I talked to Mr. Truman a lot, in my head, stoned out on kerosene fumes, looping through twenty-odd years of pickup trucks and Presidents, while I (scrape, daub, wipe) whacked away at the rust and corruption on the undersides of the truck. Never a dialogue; he never answered back, I was never that far gone in my musings. I also talked to Wendell Corey, Bobby Lane, Mrs. Tip-Top Wonder Bread, Johnny Weissmuller, people like that. But Truman was the best, the richest source, a sure bet to pull my head back twenty years and set it pinballing through the decades, bonking off the bumper bars and lighting up the lights.

I never deliberately set out on that trip; I would just start to work, scraping away at components that I knew were obsolete, and the first thing I knew I was back in the fifties, fixated on Harry S. Truman. He was not the ghost of the machine, but the ghost of the years of the machine. Then — well into the middle stages of my truck project — that ancient, silent wisp who had been Harry Truman got sick, hung on longer than was decent, and finally died. The night I couldn't get the kingpins out of my truck. I don't even want to think about what that meant.

Still, the closest that truck ever came to giving off a vibration that I could read was in reminding me of our thirty-third president. Every time I went near it. So I named the truck *The Harry S. Truman*, but I never told anybody.

CHAPTER 6

Different Strokes
for Different Folks

I'VE GOT to get serious about this. There is that leaky boulder of a truck engine lying in the middle of the barn floor, and it is the focal point of my attentions to the truck, isn't it? Because, well, it's the biggest piece. I mean it's just where one starts. Heart of the beast. Most apt (a) to be bad to start with, since that's where all the wear takes place and nobody takes decent *care* of anything anymore and (b) to break down later if it isn't put right. More stress and strain, more possibilities for gross mistakes, more expense. Requiring the most careful precision assembly, the considered application of the most arcane rituals of mechanical restitution, and all that.

All that is wrong. The engine is the only part of the automobile that most shade-tree mechanics really understand, the one aspect of automobility that has been done to death. The minimum that is really required is a kind of ballpark approximation of running order, reasonable alignment of the internal organs, and enough running clearance. The holes stopped up, the leaks plugged. Then give it enough lubrication, and don't turn it too fast, and it'll most likely run. Maybe even a considerable distance, thumping out a dependable kind of power, hanging in there. If you don't ask too much of it.

Engines are cheap. I could order a guaranteed used 1960 Dodge engine, in running condition, from a mail-order outfit for $150 f.o.b. Chicago. Sears, Roebuck sells remanufactured engines — mostly late model — starting at about $200.

A remanufactured engine is very likely better than a new engine. Sears, for example (or rather, an independent firm that does the work for Sears), dismantles the engine completely, boils out the block in various cleaning baths, inspects the parts electromagnetically for cracks and flaws, regrinds, recenters, realigns, balances, and hones everything that is still usable, and replaces everything else with new parts. New-car assembly lines operate on the assumption that since all the parts are new, the tolerances are close enough. The remanufacturer, on the other hand, must fit carefully, old to new. It is a different working stance. The assembler of new engines takes parts out of a bin and puts them into the block in front of him, just like the boss told him to. The remanufacturer necessarily exercises choice, selects carefully, measures, aligns, fits. He doesn't have a dealer network between him and the irate customer when something goes wrong. He also doesn't have a ten-million-units-per-year production schedule pushing him into short cuts.

It is remanufacture that I propose, because I want to know what is in my truck's engine. The ballpark assembly, lumping along in semidependability, is probably good enough for any purpose to which I will ever put the truck, but that's not the point. The point is to see what's in there, to understand it. To take my own head from paper theory to practice, to know what internal combustion power means — in the direct sense, via the fingertips. And the engine *is* the starting point, what must work to make the truck go, the noisemaker. The power source; yes, I will start with that, as surely as the first frustrated step in attempting to deal with a balky car is to open the hood. (Expecting to see . . . what? Blood? Broken bones?)

So I tackled my leaky boulder. Walked around it a couple of times, gave it a grunting shove this way and that to slide it maybe three inches across the garage floor. Took an idle swipe with the putty knife here and there, curling away an inch-thick icing of grease. Unscrewed the sparkplugs, took off various accessory mounting brackets, linkages, remaining small parts. Just kept going over it, taking off all the little protuberances, paring away until there was nothing left but basic engine: head, block, and pan.

And finally, unable to find anything else superficial to divert myself with, I worked my way around the corners loosening the head bolts, one turn at a time to relieve the pressure gradually. Removed all twenty-one of them. Tapped the corner of the head with a mallet to break the seal. Lifted off a thirty-pound slab of cast iron: the cylinder head. Felt in a mischievous way that I was taking the engine's cherry, but it was maybe the third engine that that old pickup had had, and God knows where that

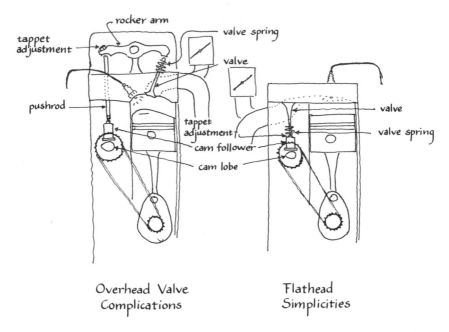

Overhead Valve
Complications

Flathead
Simplicities

engine had served before it got into my truck, how many times it had
been torn down. More like *my* cherry, engine-wise.

Slab of iron is exactly the term. Cylinder heads for overhead valve
engines are complex affairs, but this old Dodge is a "flathead," and the
term is perfectly apt. The head of a flathead engine is simply a lid on the
cylinders, a bulwark of iron to contain the explosions in the cylinders, so
that the power generated has something to set its metaphorical shoulders
against as it pushes the pistons down, turning burning hydrocarbons into
miles per hour.

The head has passages cast into it for coolant, for the sparkplugs, for
mounting bolts. It also has vestigial combustion chambers, low domes
routed into the surface to cap the cylinders and allow for the flow of
gases to and from the valves. But that's all, and in casting terms it's not
much. Otherwise, it is a plank of cast iron. I searched carefully with
putty knife and droplight, looking for cracks. Put it aside. Later I would
scour the carbon out of the low combustion chambers, but other than that
there is nothing to *do* to the head of a flathead. Take it off, make sure it
doesn't leak — that it is, in fact, flat — and put it back on. Imaginative as
a hammer.

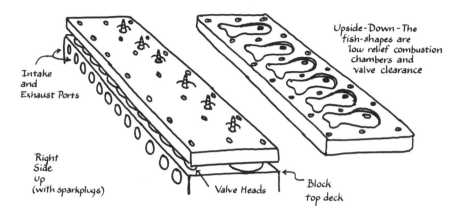

Flathead Cylinder Head – imaginative as a hammer

That left me staring down into six cylinder holes, each filled to a different level with piston. Six scorched, grubby, unhealthy-looking piston crowns. Twelve valve heads beside them, similarly discolored and loaded with carbon, in various positions from full open to tightly closed. Couldn't tell if any of them were burned. No signs of cylinder-to-cylinder leakage from a blown head gasket. Nothing to get *at*, at this end, the top of the engine.

So, upend it to get at the bottom. But do it in two stages, pausing to pull the pan off first, so whatever evil secrets it contains won't go dripping into the main bearings and other internals when the engine is bottom-end up. The oil pan was so filthy externally that I had to dig with a pocketknife even to find the bolts around its periphery. Inside was worse. The pan is only a flimsy oil storage tank, of no mechanical significance. But it hangs there underneath the engine catching the total residue, the effluvia and distillations and washed-down dirt and metal shavings of a lifetime of engine use. Draining the oil regularly only taps the top level of the filth. There was three quarters of an inch of what can only be described as oil-soaked clay and metal filings caking the bottom of the oil pan of my old Dodge. The oil filter was worse — there had been no filter element installed for the previous God knows how many thousand miles, so that accessory had gathered an even deeper accumulation of the same resinous gunk.

Thus my point about the essential stolid dependability of engines, particularly older ones: this was a running truck, capable even of generating a modest amount of oil pressure. Awash in uncirculatable, tarry, nonlubricating shit. One envisions, when thinking of automobile engines, superprecision delicacies dancing about at the leading edge of technological sophistication. Most of them, in actuality, are loose-kneed heat pumps that pay a huge tribute to the metallurgists who came up with the component alloys, and to the efficacy of modern lubricants. And almost none to the mechanical sophistication of the industry.

Anyway, cleaning out that pan, I was depressed.

Pan out of the way, the main and rod bearings were exposed, the bottom end of the engine. I unbolted a rod bearing cap, and pushed the rod and piston further up into the block. Thought I'd just go ahead and pull out one rod and piston assembly to see what it looked like. Felt the piston and rod come to a stop when there didn't seem to be any reason to. Gave it a soft tap with a plastic mallet. Was rewarded with the tinkling sound of broken piston rings, as the top ring was driven past the ridge on the upper cylinder wall.

That ridge is a good index to cylinder bore wear. It marks the highest point that the upper ring reaches on each stroke. Above it, no wear; below it, symbolically, just how much of the engine has been used up. Of course I was planning to get that ridge reamed away before putting the engine back together. Any fool can plainly see that's necessary. I also knew that the pistons were not to come out the top end, else I would break piston rings, driving them past that ridge. I'd read it somewhere. Slipped my mind in the passion of disassembly. So all right, I knew I would be putting in new rings anyway, and maybe even pistons. All part of the plan. It was just that I didn't like being stupid.

As in the fan-belt pulley. There is a stone-simple arrangement for pulling the fan-belt pulley off the end of the crankshaft. Two threaded holes in the pulley itself, into which one screws the bolt ends of a special pulling tool, tightens and the whole thing pops right off. I missed the holes first go-round and tried a different kind of pulling tool — the kind I had on hand — which put its pulling force at the rim of the pulley instead of at the shaft. That meant the pulling force only caused the pulley to

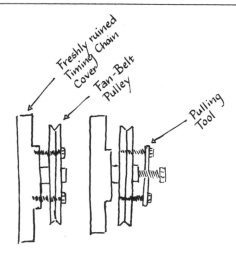

Freshly ruined
Timing Chain
Cover

Fan-Belt
Pulley

Pulling
Tool

Jerome Method —
no special
tools needed.
Three months'
parts search

Approved Method —
$ for Pulling Tool.
Timing Chain
Cover lives!

bow forward, clamping down harder on the shaft. So I decided that those two threaded holes were a self-contained pulling mechanism, put two bolts in them, tightened them down hard, punched two utterly destructive holes in the timing chain cover behind the pulley, and didn't budge the pulley a decimal fraction of a millimeter.

So I gave up on my complicated stupidities and went to ask an old Dodge man, who told me what to do. Get the right kind of puller, don't screw around. Five minutes with the right tool ($9.50) versus half a day of futzing around, destroying tools and engine parts. And undreamed-of problems to come in trying to locate another timing chain cover for a 1950 Dodge, on that hazy future day when reassembly, rather than disassembly, was the problem.

Special tools put my back up: they balloon the cost of rebuilding trucks, and they violate, somehow, the idea of minimum technology that ought to be involved in a twenty-odd-year-old vehicle. In this case I got stubborn, absorbed the principle (pull at the shaft, not at the rim), rerigged tools of my own to do it, and saved the $9.50. But that principle is overarched by a larger principle: competence, again. One has to acquire a basic background competence in mechanical principles, a familiarity with how, after all, mechanical assemblies are put together. Some of the principles are subtle (but mortifyingly simple once one grasps them). So I stumbled through the acquisition of those basic principles, breaking tools, making expensive mistakes, and regularly slapping my forehead in shock at my own repeated dumbness. I did learn, however, not to try hasty half-measures when a goof can lead to a three-months' parts search.

The timing chain cover and the broken piston rings were only small introductory adventures in the process of scattering that truck engine, naturally. But once I established the order — what had to come off before the next piece came out — I was able to bull ahead at a rapid rate. Timing chain and gears off the end of the cam and crankshafts. Main bearing caps off, leaky old oil seals thrown away. Then I could lift out the ponderous mechanical intricacy that is a six-cylinder in-line crankshaft. *That* chunk of metal gave me the willies.

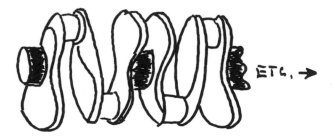

ETC, →

A lean and whippy mother — (mains shown dark)

Pause for meditation on internal combustion. If the engine is the heart of the motor vehicle, the crankshaft is the heart of the engine, and mine is a long and whippy mother, a period piece, a scary antiquity. My assumption is that it was probably a little bent, and undoubtedly had a flat rod-journal or two. The whole thing would probably have to be reground and trued if I could salvage it at all. Plymouth and Dodge passenger cars of that vintage had notoriously soft crankshafts. (A soft crankshaft wears quickly, develops flat spots, the rod bearings get loose, a rod starts knocking, and *zut!*, you are halfway to destroying your engine.) The trucks were supposedly better, but the engines were otherwise virtual duplicates, and there were a lot more passenger cars built than there were trucks. In my truck's spotty history, it was only logical that some former owner would have stumbled across a slip-fit passenger-car replacement engine, complete with buttery crank. Even if by some miracle that basic truck had remained all truck, there was still the significance of the glop in the pan, and other signs. I was not what you could call confident about the state of my crankshaft.

I wouldn't have been confident under the best of circumstances. My understanding has been warped by the horsepower race. When the engineers began looking for more horsepower in the midfifties, they went to automobile racing practices, on the theory that racing does "improve" the breed. They jumped compression ratios dramatically, squeezing the incoming gases into smaller space, containing the explosions in the cylinder much more tightly. They also expanded cylinder bores and decreased strokes to reduce internal friction, and then increased engine speeds — more revolutions per minute — by improving the flow of gases in and out of the cylinders. The engines breathed better, ran faster, churned out more power. (They also began using more fuel and pumping out more poisonous emissions. Power always costs; there is no free lunch.)

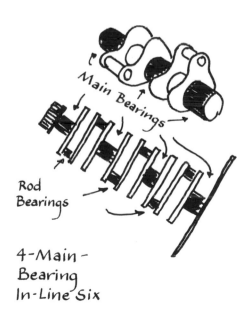

Main Bearings

Rod Bearings

4-Main-Bearing In-Line Six

These steps brought vastly increased internal pressures within the engine. With everything moving much faster, higher forces at work in every sense, the first step in maintaining some kind of mechanical order within the engine was to stiffen the crankshaft and to locate it in the most positive way possible, to hold it in absolute, vibrationless rigidity as it spun. Lots of main bearings. A main bearing on each side of every connecting rod to nail the crankshaft precisely in place. Else the hammer strokes to the tops of the pistons would travel down the rods and not only drive the crank through its appointed revolutions, but also set up microscopic vibrations, harmonic vibrations rippling up and down the length of the crankshaft, which would, unchecked, tear the engine apart.

Thus five main bearings on a four-cylinder engine, seven on a six-cylinder. One at each end, one between every two crank journals thereafter. (A V–8 can make do with five main bearings because the opposing cylinders provide a better intrinsic balance than in an in-line

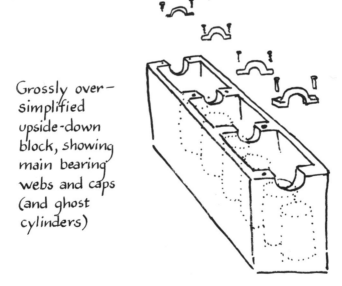

Grossly over–
simplified
upside-down
block, showing
main bearing
webs and caps
(and ghost
cylinders)

engine, and because the arrangement also allows a much shorter crankshaft. A V–8 can be the same approximate overall length as an in-line four-cylinder engine of half the displacement. Imagine the problems in the old straight-eights!) The horsepower race necessitated other tricks to help stiffen the crankshaft. Heavier webs in the crankcase to locate the main bearings more precisely. Heftier rods, rod bolts, bearing caps — and then more attention to balance to control the greater beefed-up mass. A wider use of alloys, including aluminum and magnesium, to save weight as strength was added. Bigger valves and freer-flowing cylinder heads, and lighter valve trains to reduce the inertia loads in those rapidly vibrating little metal tulips.

None of that in the era of Harry Truman, by God. Four main bearings were plenty for an in-line six. In those days when the engineers wanted more power, they simply increased the displacement. Bore 'er out — or better yet, increase the stroke. The goal was torque (low-speed pulling power, or, more theoretically, sheer twisting force at the crankshaft, ignoring considerations of speed) rather than the balls-out absolute of horsepower. Later the engineers would switch to shorter and shorter strokes to further reduce internal friction and reciprocating masses — in fact, the modern engine would commonly be referred to as a "short-stroke, high-compression" creation. But in the days of my Dodge they were after the smooth, leisurely, long-haul capabilities of torque. Long-stroke engines were naturally torquey; they produced their power at very low rpm.

Truman-era power-seekers would even go to the extreme — in modern terms — of grinding the crankshaft journals smaller, which allowed the installation of longer rods, increasing the stroke, displacement, and pulling power of the engine. That practice, by sheer reduction of the amount of steel at the crucial load-bearing surface of the journal, made the crankshaft even willowier than it was to start with. Truman-era power-seekers blew a lot of engines.

Great, long, boat-anchors of engines, which in their natural state chuffed along at their tasks, each stroke of a piston a distinct, throbbing lurch of power. Big wheels, skinny tires, long gears, ticktock slow engine speeds. To gain smoothness you added cylinders, and Sunday afternoon mechanics fussed over idle speeds, trying to balance coins on the hood just like in the legends of Rolls-Royce.

Compare that to the high-rpm whine of the modern V–8, with skyrocketing internal pressures: great power, but the power devoted to reducing time, at whatever expense in materials, costs, waste. Little wheels, fat tires, stump-puller gears for the acceleration we learned to love so well. Who cares about idle speeds: where does she peak *out?*

Stroke versus bore, torque versus horsepower, distance traveled versus time spent. The stark comparison almost seems to delineate the decades. The long, sure stroke of the "postwar" time, work to be done and we knew how to do it (unable to see where it was taking us, just wanting, eventually, to get there). Versus the volume-crazy piston flutter of the seventies, higher and higher revs — wheels spinning, peeling rubber — to stay in the same place. To be everywhere at once.

Not to worry, in the good truck *HST*. For all its 90 pounds of obsolescent steel crankshaft, a limp mechanical wand by comparison with what my late-model head tells me it should be. This truck will never have to do more than chuff along in the best 1950s style. It will contain the pressures it generates. To worry about the design concept of a crank that has already driven a vehicle to this present state of mechanical ruin — a crank that at that point of ruin was *still driving* — is silly. It is what I call my neurosis neurosis, best characterized when I find myself making lists of things to worry about, and then worry about losing the lists. All I really have to worry about is that the hoist holds when I lift that monster back into the truck . . . someday. That, and finding another timing chain cover.

CHAPTER 7

What I'm Doing
and Why I'm Doing It

BOURBON IN HAND, fire in fireplace, dog on hearth rug, cat in lap. Ache in back but glow in head. Quit early, for a little reflection: why am I doing that, out there, that puts the ache in my back?

The cat in my lap is named Boss Tweets, which stirs a thin smile of embarrassment every time I have to hand her to the vet, who keeps her records under her name, not mine. Not *my* cat, I'm not that way about cats, but after five or six years of mutually ignoring each other, she decided she is supposed to sit on my lap. I sit down, she jumps into my lap and thrashes me about the crotch with her tail, expressing irritable disillusionment, a cat's fate.

The dog's name is Blue, a hound of course, and said hound belches, regularly, with the sound of rifle fire echoing down a stone canyon in an old Gene Autry movie. We are not original in the naming of animals. I'm losing the thread here.

Quit early because of the backache. No, I quit early because my hands were too sore. Even after a couple of months of keeping at it, my hands haven't toughened up enough yet. Cuts and scratches and barked knuckles and raw patches, in and out of kerosene, wiped and wiped again to clear away enough grease to get a good grip on something else. Continual small punctures from the wicked little needles of the wire brushes. And every night the scrubbing up, gouging away around the nails and cuticles, soaking in hot water, lying in bed feeling them throb. Too stiff the next morning, fumbling at tools.

No, I quit early because I quit too late yesterday, overdosed. Aching back and throbbing hands and shit in my eyes and raw spots on my neck and the backs of my knees from stiff coveralls and nose full of stink and too cold in the barn the wood stove smoking smashed thumb boring repetitions twelve hours of solitary noncommunication too many pieces never get it done. Poor baby.

No, I quit because it tried to kill me. Pulling off all those pieces means putting the truck up on jack stands and letting it back down again, rolling it back and forth, over and over. Got a little hasty yesterday, heh heh, jacked up the front, lay down on the creeper, reached under and pulled out the stands, unthinkingly started releasing the jack to let it down before I rolled out from under. Rolling out as the truck began squshing down off the hydraulic jack. I was on my side on the creeper; the front bumper caught my upper shoulder and tried to fold my collarbones as one closes a book. It didn't have a good enough grip, and at the last moment spit me out like a watermelon seed. I coasted six feet clear on the creeper, still on my side, shrugging my shoulders back and forth to celebrate my still-intact sternum. And lay there thinking for a while.

It's just a truck.

Fixing up an old truck would be a nice hobby.

Why do I keep getting this picture of tunneling out of prison?

Chris is supportive when I quit early. She is also supportive when I overdose and quit late, although she is not beyond pointing out — not to needle, but with clear good sense — that it seems to go better when my efforts are more balanced. Chris would have me err on the side of less, rather than more, and I can appreciate that, particularly while lying on my side on the creeper, wriggling my shoulders and thinking how all that time I was worrying about the hoist failing and the engine falling there was this other garden-variety, stone-stupid disaster awaiting.

Actually, my mind was sort of blank, lying there, looking at the truck sideways. I thought for a moment about taking the jackhandle and smashing all nine of those windows, like a blacksmith taking a logging chain to the horse that kicks him. That was only a momentary impulse, but it seemed to indicate that the relationship between me and the truck was changing.

Chris can take walks. I probably misstated earlier, about juking around out in the woods. Chris does that better than I do. She generally has to lead me into it. I *imagine* it extremely well but get around to it only in connection with recognizable goals. Go see something or other. Go check how this or that is doing this time of year. I have this fantasy about somehow moseying off, simply finding myself doing it, walking about.

Ranging, really — covering a wide span of territory, just on the way to experiencing the world. But in the best of times I find myself getting purposeful about it, and recently it has become worse: to go for a walk is to launch another project. If I blamed that on the truck, I'd be projecting my own twists onto a dumb machine, wouldn't I? Chris sits still better than I do. I'm trying to learn, but the truck circumvents that kind of Zen beingness. Zen doing. The truck gets wrapped in streamers of complicated purpose.

Back there by the fireplace with the bourbon, I returned to the lemon theory. I never believed in lemons. A typewriter repairman once told me what I believed about lemons, and I never knew how clearly I believed it until he spun it out for me. There is no such thing as a machine that is fated to break or fall apart or refuse to work. Not, that is, among machines that have survived development and arrived at the mechanical adulthood of series production. If a machine doesn't perform properly because it doesn't have the proper parts, one finds the missing parts and installs them, and if it doesn't perform because the parts aren't hooked up right or are maladjusted, then one corrects the hookup or the adjustment and the lemon is cured. To believe otherwise is to reinvent demons. Machines are rational processes, with rational ailments. No such thing as a lemon, I say, crossing my fingers and knocking on wood.

I have never loved things, as things. I don't mean by that that I am superior to material pleasures. I will sucker for a new gadget as quickly as anyone and regularly convince myself that if I only had a better gizmo or new whatsis, then all this confusion and irresolution in life would clear up. But I have always been strangely — coldly — immune to affectionate relationships with faithful possessions. I sold the old Volvo after 102,000 superbly dependable miles and let it go without a tremor (Chris was sad). I will carry a pocketknife for ten years, lose it, and buy a replacement regretting only the wasted money. There's not an implement on the place that I use with any other estimation than a cold-eyed judgment about how well it works. I'm sorry about it, but that seems to be the case.

I thought I started rebuilding this truck because I needed a truck. Then I thought I was doing it to thumb my nose at the excesses of the modern motor vehicle. And then I thought — notice how the rationales become gaudier as I get further from an old truck sitting in the driveway and deeper into a barn full of junk parts — that my truck-building was a political act in revolt against the technocracy.

The politics of technology. There's an argument to be made. Archaic building codes that prevent one from forming his or her own living space, pushing the shapes one lives within to rectangular, right-angle conformity. That wed one's life and time inextricably to medieval construction methods, wasteful of both raw materials and human energy — or that surround one with the ersatz. Two-hundred-dollar appliances that sport fatal flaws in thirty-five-cent parts, requiring consultation with $12/hr. mysto-technicians who speak the magic language of the machine. The deliberate encapsulation, impenetrability, of the over-technologized things with which we furnish our lives. All these appliances that don't work very well, that mysteriously die, that involve technologies from which we have removed ourselves.

Imagine — heady dream — never again to have a gizmo fizzle, a gadget fail. Never to have another mysterious black box stop functioning, leaving you with no alternative but to take the black box in and exchange it for another, equally mysterious. No dependence on hidden technological entrails, no more puzzled moments staring at the dead appliance, the silent — and sealed — black box.

I thought I would break through all that. I would no longer be alienated from the gadgets in my life, no longer be alienated *by* the gadgets. I would keep what I understood — and could repair — and winnow out the rest. First blow, in this gadgetary revolution: against the largest appliance of them all, the motor vehicle. Thus the choice, in trucks, of an obsolete model. It had to be mechanical simplicity reduced to its essence, and I would pare it further in the process of coming to understand it. Understand it all. Know thy gadgets: first step in restoring some kind of wholeness to one's life.

And *then* I thought (fire glow cooking the denim of my pants leg to stiffness, aches melting) maybe I was just lonesome for a lovable machine. Maybe recessed in some Freudian kink underneath all my rationales, I had decided that I failed to attach myself even to the most faithful of implements for lack of knowing. Maybe I was jealous when Chris was sad about selling the Volvo; if I didn't regret the loss, then the pleasure of having it was diminished. Maybe things failed me because I never invested enough in knowing them, so they remained as character-less and emptily symbolic as currency. Mere money. And so maybe I could force myself deeply enough into the good truck *HST* to break through this uncaring isolation. Maybe that was the way — by knowing every nut, lock washer, and cotter pin, by knowing the very backside of every coat of paint — I could have a machine that had some meaning to me. Me, poor lonely child of technology, without a single truck to love so far. Poor baby me. Ah, such pompous psychological bullshit. Bourbon'll do that to you.

Well, anyway, watch it, Dodge Series B-2-B #82210917: your ass is a grape. Knock it off with the cheap-shot crusher act. You can't kill me. I will stroke you and pet you and lave you inside and out, I will clean and prettify you and set you before the world my own precious darling, but on the way I am going to finger your very fundament. I will plumb your depths. I'm going to have you. Lovingly, I hope. I'm going to know you. Biblically, if that's the way it has to be.

Besides — if I can do it, then (I think) I will be competent.

CHAPTER 8

Hostage to the Techno-Kings

Adjust valves here?

THE VALVES had come out first, of course, when I started wrestling with the engine block. A flathead's valves are flush with the top deck of the block when they are closed, but they are never all closed at once, and moving the block about while it is upside-down would damage the exposed valve heads. To get at the other end of the valves — the stems, springs, and keepers — there are two inspection plates in the side of the block. When everything is back in place in the truck, these inspection plates will be beneath the intake and exhaust manifold, which means they will also be buried beneath the carburetor linkage and attached garbage, the emergency brake cable, and various other forms of impedimenta.

To adjust the valve gap when the engine is running in the truck, I will have to drape myself over the right front fender, reach down through all those linkages and things, somehow avoid touching the burning-hot manifold and exhaust pipe, remove the two inspection plates, and, by feel, find the valve stems. The valve stems, tappets, and cam followers will be hopping up and down like . . . valve tappets. Nevertheless, I must manage, still by feel, to place two wrenches on the adjusting nuts, break

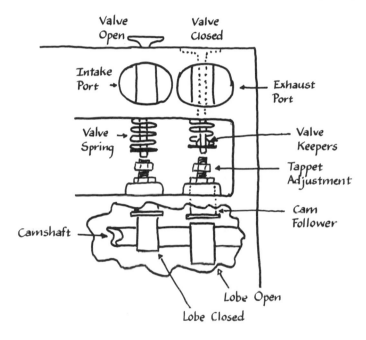

the nuts loose, and insert a feeler gauge (.010 inches for intake, .014 inches for exhaust, which means I also have to know which valve is which and which I'm working on at the moment, despite the lack of visibility and the oversupply of jiggling motion) into the gap between tappet and valve stem. I will then make a fine judgment about relative tightness and move the proper adjusting nut accordingly. Holding that judgment and that adjustment, still draped over the fender, still searing elbow flesh every now and then on the exhaust, still working totally by feel, everything I am trying to work on and make judgments about still galloping up and down like valve tappets — I will tighten everything up, locking the adjustment. Then check with the feeler gauge to see if anything slipped while I was tightening. And do it all over again if it did slip.

Only twelve of them to do. I contemplated this aspect of truck-rebuilding with mild despair as I disassembled the valve system. I foresaw that I would be adjusting valves in New Hampshire midwinter. Outdoors, as I couldn't run the truck in the barn without gassing myself. The prospect led me to more thought on the subject of competence. If the valves are not adjusted properly they will get bent (if too loose) or burned (if too tight). If they get bent or burned, I will have to do a valve job, which means a repetition of a large part of the engine disassembly process.

(Wrong, all wrong. Elbow told me later that the secret is to remove an inner fender panel and wheel, jacking up the right front corner of the truck and crawling virtually within the engine compartment to see what I'm doing and reach the valves without third-degree burns from the exhaust. I tried it, and there's room. I left the fender panel off, to be reinstalled after the engine is running and the valves are adjusted.)

Getting the valves out is easy enough: compress the valve spring sufficiently to free the keepers, pop loose those little circular wedges that grip the valve stem, and everything comes tinkling out. Push the valves up out of the block, and slip them into a piece of lath with holes drilled in a line along the length, so the order isn't mixed up. (Each stem has worn its own valve guide to fit, and if number three goes back into number five hole, there will either be severe oil blow-by or a stuck valve.) Then begin spooning the incredible collection of gunk out of the valve galleries, after the pan the filthiest part of the engine internals.

The camshaft comes out next, slid carefully out the front end of the block. A strange device: a long, skinny, solid billet of good steel (the hot rodders call them "sticks") with four carefully machined bearing journals to hold it straight and let it spin freely, and twelve eccentric lobes arrayed around the circumference. Each lobe is a pointed finger, signaling its own private valve precisely when to open and how long to stay that way. Cam grinding is a science in itself (or a mystic art, as sometimes practiced). Power-seeking engineers fiddle with lobe shapes, looking for new ways within the finite limits of a single revolution of the camshaft to hold the valve open longer, to allow more unburned gas to

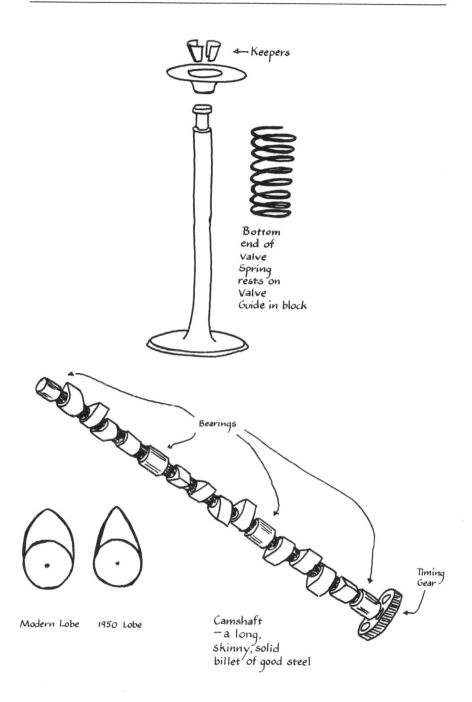

← Keepers

Bottom end of Valve Spring rests on Valve Guide in block

Bearings

Timing Gear

Modern Lobe   1950 Lobe

Camshaft — a long, skinny, solid billet of good steel

flow into the cylinder, to give more time for the burned gases to be
withdrawn. And yet still to seal the cylinder off completely, to contain
the jolt of the power stroke. This leads, on modern engines, to fat lobes,
high shoulders, microscopic variations to cut fine the compromises
entailed in each 360 degrees of revolution. But on my stolid old Dodge,
the lobes are simple teardrops. Time enough, at the rate that engine
turns, to get those jobs done.

✶ Cam out, valve train out, crankshaft out. Pull the pistons and rods,
throw away the mangled rings. I pushed the pins out of the pistons,
slipped them off the rods, numbered them with punch marks on the piston

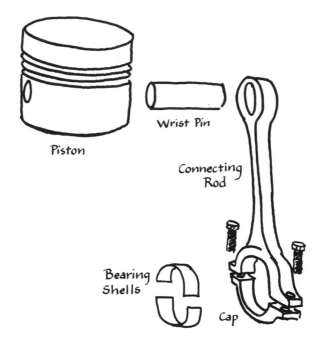

Piston

Wrist Pin

Connecting
Rod

Bearing
Shells

Cap

skirts, replaced the pins to keep the right pins with the right pistons.
Slipped the bearing halves out of the rods and replaced the caps —
already numbered to match at the factory. Pulled off the last of the little
bits, oil pump, oil-pressure relief valve, various seals. Scattered. The
engine was as apart as I could get it.

Back to the droplight and putty-knife routine, scrape and wipe, but this time for inspection rather than sanitation. It was time to see if the engine could be saved. Along about here, my friend Ned came by. Just visiting.

Ned was almost a dentist, almost a political scientist, and was a film maker for a while; now he carpenters a bit and plays a little noncommercial guitar, and lives in northern New Hampshire. Ned *is* competent — he rebuilt his house, can run a surveyor's transit, keeps his chain saw sharp — but he can't keep a car running, owing mostly to a bad habit of running off the road. I don't think he cares very much; I tried to get him going once on the subject of competence, but he dismissed it as a machismo hang-up. He was very enthusiastic about the idea of rebuilding the truck and had even helped me look for one to buy. Now that I think of it, he's the one who put me on to Elbow.

Ned settled onto the back of his neck on the red-and-white plastic truck seat, which I had stored against one wall. He had his guitar on his lap. I was turning the bare block this way and that, working along in quarter-inch increments, wiping and looking, swinging the droplight from side to side to change the shadows. Looking for cracks, galls, unusual wear spots of any kind, peeling away old gasket sealer to get at shiny metal. Inspecting.

"Hey, man, what are you doing?" asked Ned.

"I'm getting ready to hand my engine over to the Techno-Kings," I said. One does not accomplish much with straight answers with Ned.

"Right," said Ned, and fished a three-quarter-inch socket from my toolbox. He slipped it over a finger on his fret hand and started rasping out a jangly slide-guitar version of "Amelia Earhart." He stopped in midchorus. "What does that mean?"

"Well, I'm trying to find out if this block is any good. If it's worth saving. If it is, I'm going to ship it off to a machine shop and have them get it ready to rebuild."

"Far out," said Ned, working back into a softer chorus. Stopped again. "What d'you mean, 'any good'? It was running, wasn't it?"

"It was barely running. It wasn't what you could call strong. It could still be running and be busted. Something just about to let go. Put it back together that way and I'd be in deep shit."

"Right," said Ned. "What could be busted?"

"Lots of things. Hairline cracks in the top of the cylinder walls or in the bearing webs. Leaks in the water jacket. Extra wear because the crank or rods are out of alignment. Dozens of things that could be wrong. I just read a book about it."

"What's a bearing web?" Ned asked.

I turned the block upside-down and showed him the internal buttressing that locates the main bearings which in turn locate the crankshaft. I showed him the ridge in the cylinders that broke the rings when I pushed the piston out. "If nothing else, I've got to get that ridge reamed out. And I've got to get the crank measured and turned — if I put it together with a flat crank it won't last five hundred miles."

Ned went back to picking for a while. "I guess that's why they get the priests to bless the fishing boats," he said.

"Why's that?"

"Well, the fishermen over in Nova Scotia, when they do an overhaul on their fishing-boat motors, they just pull them apart, do a valve job, put in new rings and bearings, and button them back up. That's what I thought an overhaul was."

"It is, but that way is half-ass," I said, revving up my rhetoric. "Look, there's too much to do to leave it at that. You have to measure the main and rod journals, just to find out what size bearings it needs. You need micrometers and dial indicators and all that stuff, a couple of hundred bucks' worth of measuring instruments for all the things that need checking. As long as they're measuring the crank, they might as well make sure it's straight. As long as they're going to ream that cylinder ridge out of the tops of the cylinders, they might as well check cylinder bore and taper — because you can't tell if the old pistons are still good, or what size new ones you need, until you do. You need to measure pistons, check valve and lifter guides for wear, check rod alignment. You can't tell those things with the naked eye."

"Sounds complicated."

"It is. And if I don't get all that done, I'll be putting new parts back in with the old. The new parts will be stock, standard tolerances, and the old will be worn. If you don't adjust for that wear, it'll wear all over again faster than before — or tear itself apart. The least I can afford to do is to get the crank ground back to roundness. And take a little milling cut off the head and the block to be sure they're flat and mate up properly. If I don't do that, it'll blow head gaskets every time I turn around."

"I can see that." Plink, plink on the guitar again, this time "Mother Nature's Son." "You got any beer?"

"Yeah, I think there's some in there. Bring me one too."

He came back from the house with two beers and settled again against the wall. Silence for a while. "I guess that's why the priests bless the fishing boats. Particularly if you can't see all that stuff with the naked eye." Ned is not one to leave an idea alone until he's finished with it. "So what you're doing is having this truck restored."

"No I'm not," I said, scraping harder. "I'm just trying to rebuild it and make it a good, strong, working truck. 'Restored' sounds like those guys who try to rebuild exact replicas, trucks just the way they originally came off the assembly line. I'm not trying to do that. I just want to get it *right*. Solid. Dependable."

"But you're letting those guys with the micrometers do it for you. I thought you were talking about doing it all yourself."

"I *have* to. It takes a whole machine shop, thousands of dollars' worth of machine tools."

"Or you could get the priest to bless it," Ned said, grinning. "Old Elbow hauled his firewood with it. He kept it running."

"Shit," said I. "It was running, but when I brought it home the brake lines snapped off in my hand, there was two inches of mud in the sump, the steering was so screwed up you couldn't keep it on the road. There was no telling who that truck was going to kill next."

"Maybe *that's* why the priest should bless it," Ned said, and began whanging away at "Shinbone Alley." He left soon after that, but I couldn't halt the discussion in my head. I had been caught out, somehow, in violation of hippie ethics. There is a gross contradiction, I thought, in the way these people are dipping in and out of technology. Like the organic-food vegetarian who will ingest any chemical that will get him high. I am not so sure I am proceeding differently. I keep twisting the argument as I scrape at the block.

We'd had the discussion before. I was not, I had told Ned, any crazier about what technology seemed to be doing to us than he was, but I wasn't sure I could be rigid about it. There were times when it stopped being hypothetical. I used the example of when my well went dry and I'd had to haul water. (Ned had helped; it was not fun.)

Faced with the problem, I could choose to haul water from the spring by the mouthful, the cupful, or the bucketful. Opting for the technological solution — pail preferable to cup, cup better than mouth — is not simply more rational, it is more humane. I could carry water for others. It is liberating. I could carry enough for multiple uses. It is efficient: it saves resources, even if only in my food requirements. Haul buckets to save beans; feed the starving whoevers.

Okay, Ned had said, he'd take on that argument. Maybe it is easier to use the pail. But where did the pail come from? What did I have to do to get the pail? Does using the pail free me for anything else besides working to pay for the pail? What about the pail factory? What about the resources and energies used in making the pail, and the waste products, and the effect on the land of building a pail factory, and the effects on the lives of the people who work there?

Shit, Ned, I think I said, it wasn't a pail, it was just an old milk bucket we found out in the barn, you remember.

It goes on. He does the one about every technological solution creating a dozen more technological problems, about how for every infertile acre made fertile, five fertile acres somewhere else are exhausted of their resources, about destruction of ozone layers and melting of ice caps and raising of salt levels in irrigated farmlands. He gets full-throated and moist-eyed about a barn raising he went to, where he carved oak pegs with a drawknife to peg the timbers together, and they raised 20-x-20-foot frames with pikes and hand labor, just like in the eighteenth century. I've heard him do that number.

I opine that that is technology too and can accurately be located on a metaphorical straight line that stretches from the club in the caveman's hand to the moon shots. And arbitrarily to bounce back to a chosen point on that line and call it moral is sophistry. He says we have to *stop* this technological juggernaut; yeah, I say, but we won't. We'll go for the pail over the cupful.

I'd prefer to do his side of the argument — it is closer to what I had in mind when I started the truck. But the reality here in the barn intrudes, and I find myself becoming secretive. I didn't dare tell Ned about the wiring harness, for example. First step on the road to hell, sending that out to be replaced.

I had no prior experience with electrical systems. I was determined that I would come to understand automotive electrics before I was done, but I lacked confidence. I wanted to start clean, with workable basic materials, and tracing leaky circuits through rotten wiring to and from doubtful components seemed a poor way to begin my electrical education. So I rooted out that rope of rotten wiring, one end of the truck to the other, and shipped it off to North Olmsted, Ohio, where a man who calls himself "The Wire King" would turn it into electrical sanity.

Gorgeous workmanship at an outrageous price. The Wire King is a citizen who has taken on a technical difficulty, broken down its specific parts, trained employees to perform the specifics, "rationalized" (taken the fun out of) the process of rebuilding automotive wiring, and thus put a protective web of scarcity around his product. Artificial scarcity, but artificial only because nobody else wants to tackle the tedious, painstaking job — and then risk producing shoddy work with half-baked skills. Of *course* The Wire King is a Techno-King; look at the name he chose for himself.

And I was now hostage to him. Failure of courage, failure of concept. Fix the truck right, or I'd find my life devoted to the bloody thing, forever tearing it down and building it back up, getting at those parts that couldn't accommodate my guesses as to the thousandths of an inch. ("A difference of a tenth of an inch, and the Heaven and Earth are found apart" — T'sen T'saing.) Original sin compounded: I would box up the parts and cart them off to the machine shop.

If I could find a machine shop. The nearest with the capability to do the work was in Concord, seventy-five miles away, at the headquarters of a chain of auto parts stores. That meant I could perform the whole transaction through their local outlet, if I could only talk them into it.

"Naw, we don't do machine work anymore," the local manager told me. "We used to, but we lost our shirts at it. Somebody was always sending down an engine for a couple of hundred bucks' worth of machine work and then never picking it up. We've still got a seventy-one Plymouth engine out back with a bill for two hundred thirty-five bucks on it. The guy phoned in, found out what he owed, and that's the last we ever heard of him. We quit doing machine work." Which meant, roughly translated, that nobody rebuilds engines anymore. I was pursuing a dead art. The guy with the Plymouth found a used engine in a junkyard wreck, undoubtedly far cheaper than he could rebuild his own after the touch of the machinist's hand. The $235 tab just told him to look for a cheaper way.

Auto parts stores not only don't want to do machine work — despite that fully equipped shop back at headquarters — they don't want to sell parts. That is, they want to sell assemblies, bolt-ons; they want to exchange black boxes for you. They have the new-car-dealership mentality: anyone who tries to *fix* anything is an unpatriotic drag on the economy. Replace, don't fix. Perform surgery at the largest possible assembly point, and transplant. They sell units, not parts. And the closest thing to a machine tool on the premises is a cash register.

Visions of a ring of shrinking skills fill my head. Twenty years ago the corner filling-station guys rebuilt engines — including old Dodge truck engines — in their spare time. Then the availability of skills pulled back to the bigger shops, car dealerships, and independent garages. A lot of the independents used to have most of the machine tools; now you're lucky to find a garage that can even balance wheels. They're too busy hauling new assemblies from the auto parts store. I imagine a day when there will be one crusty old man left, surrounded by micrometers and machine tools in some Detroit suburb, the last man alive who can grind a crankshaft. We can pump out new engines — from automated assembly lines, untouched by human misjudgment — more cheaply and more quickly than we can fix the old. A 1950 Dodge engine? Forget it. Throw it away. The automobile engine as black-box component.

I persevered, since I was otherwise trapped. I cajoled, politicked, played the zany eccentric, tried to make friends. Finally I laid down a $50 deposit against my future unfaithfulness and persuaded the parts shop to accept, with grave reservations and emphatic denials of future responsibility, my archaic tombstone of an engine block. As far as they were concerned it was utterly useless, but they decided to humor my money.

Then I went home feeling as if I'd been trading with South Africa or something — and, of course, the Techno-Kings weren't too happy with me either, since the task I'd gotten myself into wasn't rational enough by half for their slide-rule tastes. Listen, I kept muttering to myself, I didn't get into this in order to step on *everybody's* ideology.

In fact, shipping off those parts put me in a deep funk. Ned was still nagging.

The problem with the barn raising is that Ned and friends go at it as a religious ceremony when in fact it is a technological exercise. Ned is saying, look, we can make a barn without nails, power saws, or aluminum siding. We can make a barn out of love, fellowship, human energy, and scrap trees. Fine. But not so very different, when you get right down to it, from making a moon landing out of titanium alloy, unlimited computer time, and five billion dollars. Subtract the differences in intent: a place to store hay versus nationalistic exhibitionism (with a little dubious scientific research thrown in to sweeten the budget meetings). Remove the artificial ground rules — the severe limitations of natural materials and archaic methods versus the severe limitations of a human payload and protection and return thereof — and both trips boil down to a remarkable similarity. Demonstrations of ingenuity. Technological showcases, whatever the difference in intended audience. God, I really *hate* making this argument.

I love the barn-raising idea. I imagine doing it without rulers or squares. Any measure will do so long as we all use the same one: mark off a stick to be the homemade community ruler. Work out the geometry with strings and pegs; re-create just what we need (just precisely that, and not a particle more) to raise a sound, *true* (in every sense) structure. Handsaws, axes, adzes, shakes and pegs. Beautiful. An Amish approach: thou shall not corrupt with nuts and bolts, electricity, or internal combustion. Abolishing modern technology as a holy act. I can dig it.

Imagine how busy *those* heads would be, re-creating archaic technology. How satisfying, how perfectly thrilling, seeing the joints match, the beams rise, the structure stand: reinventing technology on the spot. See how the antitechnology religiosity is siphoned away by the tool-using, puzzle-solving, order-seeking lust of our squirrely gray matter. Irresistible.

I despise making this argument.

I won't scrape engine parts with my fingernails when I can lay my hands on a putty knife. Even if I have to invent the putty knife. I may believe (as I do) that technology is responsible for the ecodisaster. I may think I am totally committed to resisting technology's advances, may have a firm ideological or spiritual foundation bolstering my resistance. But a putty knife works better. My fingernails would soften in grease, I'd look around for something more effective — a stick, a sharp rock, a nail — and invent the putty knife. As the sparks fly upward. (A technological principle used to warm our homes and keep the smoke out of our caves.)

Well, sure it's silly, but I've got to figure out some way to accommodate the Techno-Kings in my head.

The first mistake the Neds and I make is to fall in love with the idea of Process. Barn raising. To hell with efficiency: if you *love* making pegs with a drawknife (scrape, wipe, daub), the man from Metl-Bilt Pre-Fab Barns, Inc., will stop thumbtacking his business card to your screen door. "To the extent that one's heart and energy can go into the doing and being," another Ned wrote to me once, "into relating to the objects, the people, the process, his need of swift, efficient, easy results diminishes; the point is to find the things we enjoy doing and do them — with reverence and joy and growing strength and awareness."

Oh, I can get off on that, all right — witness all that fancy talk about scraping carbon by cozy droplight. I can get off on dishwashing (hot water, rich suds, grungy plates transformed, orderly ranks growing in the rack, squeaky clean). I can get off on blackberry picking, on shoveling shit, on nickel balsa-wood throw gliders. Once. I can't get off on water hauling anymore; I bought a very technological pump. That is, I can go head over heels for the somewhat high-flown notion of Process, but I'm not sure I have faith that it will hold off technology.

In fact I think it brings it on. If you really love making oak pegs with a drawknife, really get off on that, then you can easily forestall the impulse to buy manufactured birch doweling to peg your beams. You cannot, however, forestall the impulse to keep your drawknife sharp. You will seek better ways of sharpening it. You will speculate about, and maybe even experiment with, new blade materials, tempering processes, handle conformations. You will lay on all the technology you can to make the process of peg carving into the lovely, sensual craft that you know in your heart it can be. Something you can do with reverence and joy and growing strength and awareness.

I can't imagine anyone more deeply into Process than, for example, Enrico Fermi.

The larger mistake, however, is to assume that there is a point on that line between the caveman's club and the moon shot that marks the moral turnaround, before which technology was somehow benign, after which it is malign. Theological discussion for the College of Cardinals: Let's see now, shall we slice 'er off right before the invention of carbon steel? Naw, Giuseppe wants to keep his fish knife. How about just after the vulcanization of rubber? The moldboard plow? Ice cream? Just before the six-gun? Or is it that technology went awry when that fellow in Eden utilized the inclined wedge — his incisors — to excoriate the apple?

There are Neds who will demonstrate in exhaustive technical detail that pegged beams never split in the joints and nailed beams almost always do. Old-fashioned long-stroke Dodge engines can be tuned to give better gas mileage and produce less air pollution than "modern," "high-efficiency" V–8s. They are saying the old technology was in fact better. Technologically better. In other words, technology is bad but the old technology wasn't quite as bad because it had more technology to it. Less is more.

Foolishness, says I; I'll just resolve these inconsistencies myself, make all my own technological choices between the good and the bad. (A certain megalomania is in operation here: never mind, don't worry about me, I'll just quietly decide for myself which stream I'll dump my effluent into.) I'll rebuild this old truck and keep the *good* parts, the socially useful parts. But, ahem, I'll check with the Techno-Kings about what will actually work. Technology has its bluff in with me. I suffer from too much technology at too early an age, too much half-assed knowledge, too much respect for the old hard-line, metal-to-metal, go/no-go view of reality. My past leaves me just brain-damaged enough that to me, technology is the last absolute.

So here I sit scattering the bones of my last daddy. Result: fear. (That isn't really the reason Ned keeps talking about priests — that's a joke — but it is why I have gone in hostage to the Techno-Kings.) Weirdness. It's just a truck. It's just an old, beat-to-shit truck and I really do understand quite a bit of it. It isn't physical fear: the homicidal tendencies of the operation can be avoided easily enough, if I stay loose and careful. That doesn't bother me anymore.

But I am gnawed by fluttering anxiety over the most inconsequential mechanical fragment. That's been the emotional climate from the day I backed the truck into the barn and hung the key over the door. What causes that? Residue from childhood Christmas toys and all those adult warnings? Afraid — with parts strung over a country mile — that I will *break* it? Or afraid I will commit the irreversible technological stupidity, some error so large that this truck I don't yet have will nevertheless be permanently lost? That I will have to do it over? That when I am finished, some unimaginably diabolical unturned screw will stop me dead? That it *won't work?*

Send the scary parts off to the Techno-Kings. *They* won't break it.
Daddy fix.

*The night I sent the engine parts off, I dreamed I flew a small airplane,
controlling it with a throttle that was like an oversized light switch. I
could hear the motor buzzing away, but we were losing power; the buzz
threatened to be interrupted and then all would be lost.*

*Whatever the pronouncements of the new transcendentalists, the
greened-out New Community, power is our lives. We have the internal
combustion engine embedded, buzzing, in our consciousness. In the fifties
we drank "to get a buzz on"; in the sixties acid sizzled along our
synapses, pulling us on our trips. We have muted the hum of our real-
world machines, but when the hum fails we are disoriented. When the
dynamo stops the lights dim, the record runs down through deep bass to
silence, we are adrift. The reassuring hum resumes with our waking
moments. Buzz of "life."*

*(How acute can hearing be? Does waking mean the sound clicks on, the
buzz of bloodflow past the ears indicating that yes, the power has
returned, they've fixed the trouble, we can go on — what were you
saying?)*

*External power sources switch my life from active to passive. The hum
comes on and I can relax, let go, it is out of my hands. I am being done,
rather than doing. I am conditioned from birth to know that power is
externally applied. I construct defenses, play elaborate games of
"controlling" power. But in the end I know I will be soothed by the power
that comes from the switch, the key. The buzz will pull me where I want to
go. Where it wants me to go. Did mother's milk flow without a hum?*

*I write on an electric typewriter, making lists of buzzes. Radio and TV.
Air conditioning and furnace. Refrigerator and dial tone. Transportation, information, communication, food, clothing, shelter. We have
powered all our facilities. Now mail-order gadget houses sell "white
sound" — a humming machine to override all the other hums that might
keep us awake. Buzz over crickets, birds, dogs barking, roosters crowing.
Ultimate security blanket. Sleep soundly.*

CHAPTER 9

Hlude Sing, Goddamn

WHILE THE TRUCK PARTS were being shipped off to the machine shop, winter was grinding down out of the north woods at a steady fifteen miles per day.

There is a slash mark across the map of the northernmost peninsula of the Province of Quebec, starting in one of the deeper nooks of Ungava Bay on the east (Gyrfalcon Island marks the mouth), cutting across to the southwest, touching the northern tip of Lac Guillaume Delisle before meeting Hudson Bay. It is the "northern limit of wooded country" between longitude 70° and 75°. Although to the north of that line are hundreds of miles of Arctic shrub and to the south of it are many more miles of vestigial evergreen brush, still, it is at this point — where the woods begin — that the display of fall colors symbolically begins its march.

The foliage change depends less on weather than on changing sun angles and the life cycles of the plants involved. The signal that tips it off comes from a deeper, truer source than the rather harebrained weather patterns, which can fool a duck but won't ever fool a sugar maple. The line that marks the peak of the fall color slides down the globe like Sherwin-Williams paint. (I keep thinking of that term the astronauts use to describe the beginning of moon shadow: "terminator." Chilling mentality.) It starts at the edge of the woods in August, not quite a thousand miles to our north. It moves southward fifteen miles a day, every day, come hot rain from the Bahamas or sleet storm from the Yukon. It reaches us on the fifth of October, every year.

Of course I couldn't get any of the neighbors to agree to that date. The principal activity of the foliage watchers is to drive around the countryside during the last week of September and the first ten days of October, saying to each other, "Is this the peak? Oh, this *must* be the

peak." Chartered busloads of gray-headed ladies arrive from the cities to
the south, clotting the local restaurants and postcard counters at
noontime, mysteriously disappearing after dark. Tedious arguments
develop about when, after all, the peak of the color really *is*. The air is
filled with the sound of grinding cameras, color film being pumped
through like a river of celluloid. Drugstores and photo-supply shops
exhaust their supplies in the first week, and the personnel get nasty
thereafter at the sheer traffic, all those customers to turn down.
Invariably, sadistically, the locals, when asked about the *real* peak of the
color, will opine that it'll be along in about five days. Or a week ago.

I will straighten out this confusion. The foliage change actually starts
in early September, when you will see a single limb gone foolish in the
midst of an otherwise dark green maple, a spot of brilliant yellow or
orange flame on a monochrome hillside. It spreads quickly after that, a
flamboyant disease, the chlorophyll disappearing to expose the rich
yellow-through-purple spectrum that the botanists insist is there all
along, hiding under the green.

The color grows, sharpens, enriches, spreading through the woods and
along the roadsides, vibrating chromatic amplitudes, overrich contrasts,
God's full-volume hi-fi Bach organ music of color, all stops out. Visual
burnout. One is bombarded with color molecules; to step outdoors is like
waking in full sunlight with a hangover. Your eyes ache.

That's the *first* peak, which is one of intensity; it is for epicures,
occurring before the color change is total, while there is some green left.
It slides up the scale of bearability, approaching pain, then slips away
overnight. It runs perhaps thirty miles ahead of the second peak, which
is the peak in volume. Between one day and the next you catch a hint of
leaden sheen in the leaves, almost a blue gray aura; it isn't really there
when you look for it, just a hint at the corner of the eye, but the treble
vibrance is gone. Then the second peak is here, the hills are totally red
(fading into brown), the life sapped out, the leaves beginning to fall. The
second peak is for gluttons.

Does funny things to the consciousness when one lives in the middle of
it. I really look forward to the fall foliage, talk about it months ahead of
time, insist that friends postpone their late summer visits for the full
socko zonk. I anticipate rich American harvesttime, rough sweaters, fire
in the fireplace, all that good stuff. But the emotion I feel when I see that
first bright limbful peeking out of the green is neither celebratory

harvest joy nor sweet melancholy fall sadness: it is panic. It is too early, my blood is still running summer-grade, I am not ready yet. Ever.

The full sweep of the foliage change is disorienting, furthermore, too gorgeous to live in, staggering with its weight. It is calendar art, Hollywood sunset, showbiz. It *is* a show, and the audience that comes up from the city for twenty-four-hour doses sees just enough. Living on-stage, with all those zoomy spotlights, is what wears one out. When the leaves begin to fall, I literally sigh with relief, postfuneral; the death of the year is a lump of trauma I am goddamn glad to get over with.

Besides, some years we are given a tag-end pocket of pure relief. The previous November we had been able to enjoy an all-day outdoor picnic on the second day of the month, didn't even need sweaters until dark, and I remember sitting in the sun with my shirt off for about four hours, toasting. On the second day of November. The sharp, hard lines of the trees exposed, the shape of the land, colors muted to subtle browns and grays, the spine and ribs of the earth showing, and yet we got this daylong gift of languid ease, steaming out the dammed-up summer juices. I'd have been tempted even to try the creek, except for the rim of ice in the shady spots.

No gifts this year, of course. Coldest, wettest summer on record, according to the Boston *Globe*, and fall a continuation: solid rain between the end of the foliage and the arrival of the hunters. The woods were a sloshy mess by the time the death-jocks started coming in, which undoubtedly pulled down their collective mood somewhat. I could tell, by the surliness of the crowds in the state liquor stores.

I have tried to be tolerant about the hunters, having moved by choice to a region where I share the wilderness with them (realizing that in fact they were here first). I've killed a few animals myself, both in foolish waste and in order to eat the flesh, and I've been swept along in the sophistry that if I am going to eat meat, I should be willing to accept the responsibility of the killing. Okay, I will accept that responsibility — I just won't go seeking the experience out of "sport." But I have tried not to shut my mind against the sportsmen, the serious local food providers or the city visitors who otherwise would never blow the soot out of their systems. Who would never experience what a nice place the woods are if it weren't for hunting.

Unfortunately, my experience with hunters precludes all that nice-guy tolerance. The season opens and suddenly the shoulders of the local roads are jammed with cars and pickups, parked helter-skelter in blatant disregard for the passage of traffic. The liquor stores and bars are overcrowded with large men in Day-Glo hunting gear who are not having a good time. One sees the occasional roadside vomiter, leaning over a pickup fender, staining the snow. It would be scary enough if that were the whole story — an overload of drunks in search of some self-stimulated heroics. But they also carry guns.

We batten down and board up, stay indoors, avoid the roads. It is not only that the woods are unsafe during the nicest time of the year. It is not even safe in our backyard. I have seen stalkers emerge, heads down, from the woods thirty yards from our back window, glance up, recognize a scarcity of killable beasts, and turn their guns and plunge back into our woodlot. Creepy.

Others have worse stories to tell — hunter-blasted cows, mules, automobiles, window lights. Gun-waving threats. Our experiences haven't been bad enough to do more than make us afraid of our woods for long periods at favored times of the year. Last spring Chris and I went down for a dip and found a fearless fisherman working over our swimming hole. He sported two or three hundred bucks' worth of Abercrombie & Fitch appliances and gear, a lot of heroic clothing (in seventy-eight degree summer balm), and was teaching the intricacies of trout-killing to two boys, aged about five and seven. He had two dead four-inch fingerlings skewered on — ripped open by — a half-inch green sapling he'd torn from some of the precious greenery that shields our skinny-dipping pool from the roadway. He had about nine different tools of manhood hanging from his huntsman's-special four-inch-wide khaki web belt, including — so help me God — a pistol. To protect him from the four-inch trout, I suppose, on a gorgeously sunny May day. Oh my. The kids were very whiny.

Over in Maine they recently debated a bill requiring hunters to wear fluorescent clothing while in the woods. This seems to me to be the correct approach. I would like to suggest some additions. Perhaps all hunters should be required to wear six-inch pink satin bows on each ankle, trail a red balloon on a five-foot string tied to the belt, and wear a whirlie beanie. Or Bozo-the-clown make-up. Ought to do wonders for the mental set with which they approach the woods.

The hunters go away in late November. The days get colder and wetter, the rain occasionally turns to spitty snow, the ground freezes solid, there is a continual kind of sodden gray rot to the world. Slit-your-wrists time again, forever and ever. Then finally the low-pressure areas gather themselves appropriately somewhere in the St. Lawrence River valley, a load of moisture gets pulled up along the Atlantic seaboard to just off the coast of Maine, God puts a backspin on the whole meteorological mess and bounces it off a cold front, and *whump!* A foot of snow. A classic nor'easter.

That changes everything. The change you couldn't make in your head and body, back when you were merely threatened by winter, takes place overnight. Mostly, one . . . slows. The fidgets of human intercourse are muted, just as the hard-pack on the roads sops up most of the vibratory tire and road noise as you drive over them (before the salt). I may not have wanted winter in November, when I had the chill misery of the season without the décor. But by December — after more cold rain than I could have believed possible — I am goddamn grateful for it. Thick, soft, muffled, snow-covered, battened-down wintertime. It is time for weather conditions that can be shriekingly brutal, that can whimsically kill, but somehow, now, the pressure's off. Come inside. It's all going to work out.

All tucked in by the first snowstorm, I was happily trying to get the old Dodge oil pump to accept a new shaft and rotor out in the barn. Wood stove puffing merrily, keeping a pot of coffee hot. Windowsills loaded up with new snow to change the shape of the shadows on the floor. Early afternoon, sun just starting to work on the south side of the barn. Eaves beginning to drip. Nice place, nice time, grease to my elbows. Ned and Annie drove up.

They had new cross-country skis, which Ned had taken in payment for some remodeling work for a local ski shop. They wanted to know how to use them. Ned and Annie, and most of our local friends, scrupulously avoid ski-resort skiing. (I work at it from time to time, as a ski writer, trying to raid ski-biz for money to support a non-ski-resort life.) But ski touring — disorganized, nonmechanized, and extremely cheap — is a recent, healthy fad among this hitherto antiskiing set. So anyway, nothing would do but I should shuck off my greaser clothes, get Chris and skis, and head for the woods with them. I was not too loath.

Off we went, after twenty minutes of confusion with waxes and gear and a sack of oranges. We caught a hiking trail near the house and worked our way gently up into National Forest. A hundred yards deep in the snow-filled woods, and my God, *magic*, sharp blues and whites, transmuted shapes, burdened bush, the woods unified by this single, consistent, surreal texture: snow. Sunlight shattered, crazed, refracted into jangling spikes of light. All the visual clichés, Japanese prints and dreamscapes. We would stop to look and breathe for a moment, and twenty yards away an overloaded limb would choose that instant to dump. No wind, no bird flight, not another, additional, scale-tipping flake of snow; just this sudden, silent shower, a tree come alive in the woods. Should have made a roar but didn't; our ears all stuffed with God's own cotton. Smile at each other. Step out, slide another hundred yards, stop again. Smile. Unbearable.

We went in perhaps a mile and a half, crossed an old logging road, got tired of climbing, and turned back to follow the road downhill. Some ski tourers will set out to cover measured distances, or set a cross-country runner's pace, but we usually just walk and climb back up onto the shoulders of the mountains — not much more than a stroll, really, unless we catch the weather wrong. Then we turn around and slide back down the way we came. Go in for about an hour, ski out in ten minutes, just standing on our skis while the scenery slides past. That's what we did this time, although we followed the logging road out, rather than our own tracks. We looked for deer a lot — it is so quiet, sliding along on the skis, that we can sometimes ski right up on the wildlife, even into the middle of a deeryard in deep winter. But we didn't see any.

The logging road brought us to the county road, out of the woods, a mile or so from the house. We started talking again then, the cathedral mood over, Ned and Annie's minds just about melted from their first snow trip. It was fairly flat terrain alongside the road, but we stayed on our skis rather than walking on the pavement and carrying the gear. We played at trying to master the shuffling glide of the experienced ski tourer. The road generally follows beside the creek bed along in there, and we stopped several times to look at the creek and listen to its hidden gurgles. Just lovely. A lovely afternoon.

About halfway home, I was screwing around down in a hollow beside the creek and came to a strange, extremely regular rise, a snow-covered hillock about thirty feet high, its top level with the roadway. I tried to sidestep up on it but the skis wouldn't bite. The snow would immediately slough off underfoot, exposing plastic sheet. The whole hillock was man-made, a huge sandpile put there by the highway crews and covered with plastic, I assume, to prevent it from freezing solid. Strange that I hadn't noticed it before. The snow on top of the plastic was *very* slippery.

Ned and I both tried to climb it on skis, but kept falling and sliding down. Actually, we never made it four feet up from the level ground at the bottom. Finally Ned shuffled around the edge of it, worked his way up to the road surface, and removed his skis. Without saying a word, he took off across the top of the hillock, and about ten feet from where it started curving downward, he launched a swan dive. With a great screech of joy he disappeared into the snow a few feet from the edge, slid over the brink on his stomach, and, carrying a foot of loose snow with him on the slippery plastic surface, plummeted the thirty feet to the bottom in a single, nonstop slide.

Giggling panic. The women and I fell over one another trying to make our skis work up the edge of the sandpile, while Ned went around the other side on foot. We raced to the top, dumped our skis, and imitated Ned's flight. It was a perfect thirty-foot playground slide, a toboggan ride without need of a toboggan. It was unreal how well it worked. Annie and I headed toward, crashed into, each other, slid to the bottom entangled, upside-down and backward, scooping up armloads of snow, getting it stuffed willy-nilly under parkas, down necks, into groins. Scream and scramble for the top again. We were like twelve-year-olds off the high dive. There was no way we could hurt ourselves, no angle or attitude of launch that would not carry us in a single, swooping slide all the way to the bottom. We went berserk, mad, thrashing back up to the top at a trot, relaunching in four-person chains, wheelbarrow and dog fashion, soaring collapses, hitting the bottom and rolling over into a scrambling crouch to paw at the snow and get to the top again.

Maybe ten minutes of absolutely insane screaming, tackling, tumbling madhouse. Nonstop physical hysteria. Then we all four ended up sitting side by side in the snow at the bottom, blowing hard, struggling for breath, soaked and abraded and chapped and freezing. Ned swung his arm to indicate our hillock; behold, we had scraped it absolutely bare of snow, it was now just a pile of sand covered with plastic sheet.

We pulled ourselves back up the grooved trail we'd worn beside the hillock, slipped into our skis, and started shuffling and gliding toward home again. Nobody said a word. It wasn't far. Funny I hadn't noticed the sandpile there before though.

Hot cider and a big fire, and we put together something to eat, but mostly we just sat and steamed. Then Ned and Annie stuck their skis back in the car and drove home. I was all stoked up to take on Ned again in the philosophy of truck-rebuilding, but I didn't get around to it. As a matter of fact, I forgot.

Junkies

IN THE BEST JUNKYARD you will ever find, the office will also be the home of the owner. It will be located in one corner of the yard, a portion of its walls indistinguishable from the fence that delineates the junkyard proper. Somewhere back there in the bowels of the house will be a house trailer, vintage 1948, the essential living unit which has grown, carefully and slowly, by an accumulation of ells, add-ons, pantries, skylights, stoops, and covered walkways into home-and-office.

To enter the office is to enter the owner's home; when you are in the door you are in the kitchen, and Mrs. Owner will be sitting, in cotton housedress, curlers, white socks, and split-at-the-heel sheepskin slippers, drinking coffee at a chrome and Formica dinette set. She will be smoking long cigarettes, with longer ashes clinging to them, and she will have a very deep voice, when and if you ever hear her talk.

You will not likely hear her talk, however. It will be very quiet in that kitchen, office, trailer, home. There may well be some other people sitting in it; they will average about 200 pounds apiece, male and female, and while they may not all be drinking coffee, they will all be smoking cigarettes with long ashes on them. Nobody will say anything. There will not be a solitaire game going, a soap opera playing, not even a radio breaking the silence. It will be 9:30 A.M. on a gray and overcast late fall morning, all these people will be sitting around in straightback chairs smoking and not talking to each other, and about twenty seconds after you enter you will be stricken with a kind of nervous sweat. You will feel that the world has gone . . . strange.

Persevering, however, you will blurt out something introductory, aimed at the general group: "You have any old Dodge pickup trucks back there? I need a gas tank for a fifty model . . ." This will serve to locate which person is the proprietor, who will then tell you that he's got a '53 but the gas tank's no good, and he thinks there may be a '49 back there somewhere but you'll have to find it. This is the one statement, in an infinite universe of statements, that you want to hear. It means that you can then wander with your tools through his yard, browsing as in a bookstore. It means he will trust you, and trust from a junk dealer is absolute. If it isn't there you won't be allowed past the fence, and you will expect your car to be searched when you leave. If trust is there, you have to stop on the way out to press money on the owner for the parts you have acquired.

That is to say that there are all kinds of junkyards in the world, ranging from half-acre car piles, ignored by their collectors, in the back corner of some other kind of vaguely automotive enterprise, to well-ordered, milelong stretches of cross-indexed derelicts, sequestered by model year, body type, and state of damage. There are junkyards with Telex intercommunication systems linking them with other yards across the next several states. There are junkyards with reference libraries, or at least collections of parts manuals, guides to interchangeability of parts, and other printed aids to sorting out the bewildering proliferation of automobiles and trucks.

The big yards are veritable supermarkets of damaged automobiles. Their primary business is in body parts and sheet metal — mechanical parts are heavy, not readily inspectable for damage, and chiefly interesting to bargain hunters. The important customers are the bump shops that quote insurance repair estimates on the basis of new parts ordered from the factories, then multiply their profits by cannibalizing junkers to make the repairs. The big-turnover, high-profit items are grilles and bumpers. Décor — and the most fragile and dangerously exposed part of the automotive décor at that. (The federal regulations requiring five-mph-crashproof bumpers are going to make a gigantic change in the nature of the junkyard business.)

I don't like to deal with the large junkyard chains. I would like to be able to claim that this is because I don't like their style and prefer the down-home comfort of the small operator, but that wouldn't be entirely accurate. I really don't like the big yards because I have to know what I am doing to trade there. They are businesses, run almost efficiently, unprepared to serve my halting efforts to figure out what it is that I need. After a couple of frustrations, I learned that what I have to do is sit and stare at a part for a while. Take measurements, mull, worry. Summon up visions from the barn back home, where the part to be replaced lies broken among the cowshit. They don't have time for any of that at the big yards.

(What really helps most of all is taking the junker apart for myself, getting the feel of the process. If it feels fairly familiar — if I know where everything is — then it is a pretty safe bet that I'm getting what I need. If it is strange, if I have to figure it out, I am up the wrong tree. Also, in the disassembly one collects a lot of information — degree of rust, etc. — about the state of the piece.)

The best yard I found was a private little acre belonging to a rural Chrysler-Plymouth dealer, a collection of wrecks intended only for in-house cannibalization. The parts man let me browse, and I found a '49 pickup — very close to identical to my own truck — cocked up on one side on the lip of a draw. The yard owner was obviously using the collection of worthless junk chassis, after they had been stripped, to stop soil erosion in the draw, and my target Dodge was next in line to be pushed over the edge. In fact it was already teetering.

The problem was that I had to dig a foxhole in the soft sand and crawl underneath to get at the parts I wanted, and then cower there, oh-so-gently trying to remove pieces while the truck wavered on the edge. I had it figured that if it toppled over into the draw, it would leave me sitting in the sand on the lip. It was fairly obvious, however, that if it decided to slide instead of tip, it would carry me, sand, tools, and high-flown notions down the thirty-foot embankment to crash into the other wrecks waiting below. I didn't want to be in a car wreck in a junkyard.

Besides, the gas tank of that '49 model was even holier and more rusted than mine, and the front end was smashed in so I couldn't get at the timing chain cover — number one on my absolutely essential want list — without pulling the whole engine. I spent three or four nervous hours at disassembly, pulled off maybe a dozen minor parts that were improvements on what I had at home but which weren't really essential, and gave up. I carried twenty pounds of salvaged parts back to the parts man, bargained a bit, and paid three dollars to walk away with them. It was such a pleasant place I really wanted to go back, but there wasn't anything else on that lone Dodge truck that I needed.

Later I discovered a yard that was a reasonable match for the aforementioned Platonic Ideal of junkyards. Home-and-office combination, housedress, curlers, cigarettes, and split-heel slippers. The difference was that this one-man operation was big business. It covered twenty or thirty acres, stretched between a major highway and a railroad track, almost within city limits. The owner wasn't in the junk car business, he was in salvage, and in addition to the automobiles there were huge piles of junked refrigerators, junked well-drilling equipment, junked logging gear. Huge piles of indistinguishable scrap metal. Enough railroad timbers to redo the Trans-Siberian Railroad. The owner had *equipment:* fork lifts, cranes, heavy trucks, front loaders. He ran it himself, moving from one machine to another through the day, shifting piles of material around. There was even one stack of junk bicycles.

He was friendly and understanding, if not too optimistic about what I would find. Spoke with a slight accent that I couldn't identify. He gave me the run of the place, and I grabbed my toolbox and strode off into hog heaven, certain I would come away with pieces to rebuild half a dozen trucks. Happy hunting ground.

There were two problems with that yard. The first was that he didn't happen to have much in the way of twenty-year-old Dodge trucks, so I was making some wild guesses, as I picked through those acres of junk, about what might eventually prove useful to me. The second part of the problem was my digestive system. I visited that yard, one might say, on the wrong day.

I was about 600 yards from the office, in that forest of scrap, and halfway through removal of yet another gas tank, when I was stricken with an absolutely irresistible intestinal urge. By that time I was grease and rust to the armpits and didn't particularly care to ask for the use of the office facilities, even less to hunt for a filling station. Didn't really even think there was time. The owner was messing around in the distance with his fork lift. What the hell, I thought, let us not be delicate. So I drifted over behind a stack of 1963 Chevrolet front ends and hunkered. I was in a hurry.

In too much of a hurry to realize, until after the first spasm, that I'd neglected to cover my flanks with regard to the suddenly busy highway. So I scuttled around the corner to avoid that exposure, and found myself facing, between towering rows of rusty metal, the proprietor, headed my way on his fork lift. Back around another alleyway, duck-walking with trousers at the knees, in a growing sense of panic. Spasms. The sound of the fork lift coming my way again. More scuttling. The rasp of the fork lift from another angle. What is he *doing*, checking his fence line? Taking a tour of the place? Then another sound, carrying over the fork lift's engine noise: the unmistakable *chuff, chuff* of a train. The goddamn Boston and Maine. One little three-car train every two weeks or something like that, and here it comes, on the only unexposed side I have left. Probably carrying three carloads of Girl Scouts on a field trip. I thought the railroads were long dead.

By the time I had recovered enough dignity to face the yard operator again, I was too weak to mess around with auto parts anymore. I did take the gas tank. It had a hole in it. I bought it anyway, out of some kind of twisted embarrassment.

"Got a hole in it," the owner said.

"Yeah, I know. Have to get it welded. It's better than the one I've got at home though."

"Tough to weld, gas tanks. I dunno. Call it a dollar, then. If you can't use it, bring it back and I'll give you the dollar back."

He was a nice guy, but there was this funny little smile playing around the edges of his mouth while we were talking, and I've never quite felt like going back to that yard. I stopped at the town dump and threw away the gas tank before I got home.

I finally found my replacement gas tank at a supermarket junkyard. Had to leave my tools in the car, and they didn't even want me to see the tank before buying it. I talked them into it and rode with a yardman in a four-wheel-drive Chevy about a mile and a half over the Vermont hills to look at one old Dodge truck, in among about two dozen other pickups of similar age. Watched him use bolt cutters and sheer brutality to pull the tank off. The engine was gone; no timing chain cover. I asked about that later. "Should've been here last month," the owner said. "We sent about six hundred engines off for scrap. Probably one in that batch, if you'd known."

They charged me $10 for a dented and battered tank, but it didn't have any holes in it, so I cleaned it up and painted it and hung it on my truck. After it was installed, I realized that it was full of sediment, and I'd probably have to pull it off and flush it out somehow, but at least I had an intact tank in place. I still catch myself daydreaming about going back and sneaking into that monster junkyard with tools though. Boy, did they have a lot of good stuff.

CHAPTER 11

God Is Complexity.
Or Is It Simplicity?

IF YOU THINK about brakes very much, you may never drive again. I was not exaggerating when I recounted the condition of the brakes to Ned. The first brake line I touched snapped off in my hand, and on that old Dodge there are no safety back-up systems. When one brake line goes, zap, zero brakes. (A good reason for the separate, mechanical parking-brake system working on the drive shaft, if I could make it work.) All four wheels were wet with leaking brake fluid from the wheel cylinders, which turned out to be full of some indescribably gunky mixture, semifluid, definitely not brake juice. And like that. I really don't understand what was stopping the truck.

So presto, the compleat brake job, no sooner said than if I can ever find my way into the back drums I'll be with you in a jiffy, ma'am, just as soon as my hernia stops smarting. The rear drums are a jam-fit on a tapered steel axle, with an inch-and-a-quarter nut tightened to about 700 foot-pounds of torque. What all that hot-shot technical talk means is that I need a *big* hammer to get the mothers off. In fact I need a big puller, the kind with ears to beat on with my big hammer. I resisted this item — cost $17 — for about ten days. I banged on those rear brake drums with a lot of various-sized hammers, invented stop-gap puller gadgets, even used a butane torch to try to expand some metal enough to force things loose. Ten days of escalating despair, then a $17 purchase in a fit of temper, and I was ready for a brake job. Convinced that a cleverer mechanic could have worked it out without the special tool. Christ, I get stubborn sometimes.

Brake drums off, the beauty of a complete teardown swept over me. It's so much easier to go ahead and do the whole thing instead of patching

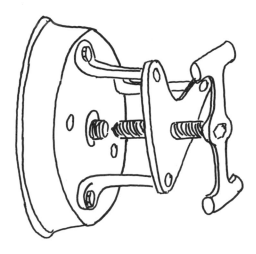

Brake Drum Puller
Rear ($17)

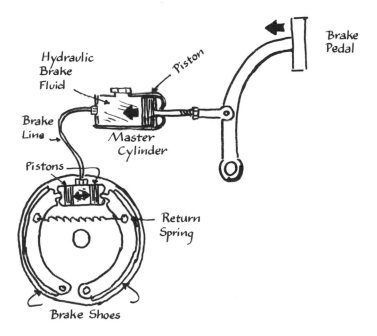

into a busted system, never sure that what's upstream isn't also rotten. I stacked the drums to one side, then worked my way around the truck with a big washtub, letting everything simply fall into the tub — nuts, bolts, washers, springs, pistons, wheel cylinders, the works. Fished out the brake shoes, which are to be replaced anyway, then covered what was left with solvent. Some rubber parts in there that the solvent isn't particularly good for, but they too are to be replaced. Clean everything once, then mix and match, building four wheels' worth of brakes from the tubful of pieces.

Celebrate with me the lead-pipe simplicity of hydraulic brakes, for which parts are available and cheap, causes of failure easy to locate, and fifth-grade physics sufficient. I step on the brake pedal, which pushes on a piston in the master cylinder. The piston applies pressure on brake fluid, through steel tubes — brake lines — leading to all four wheels. At each wheel, a wheel cylinder, with its own pistons, which in turn press the brake shoes out to rub on the brake drums, slowing the wheel. The car stops. Safe again.

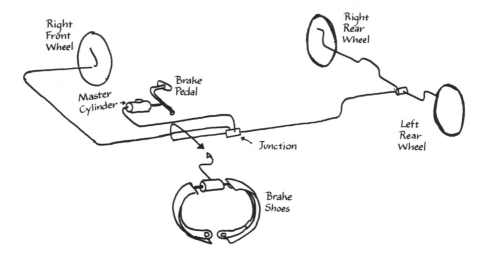

I even pulled off the brake pedal and painted *it*, in my no-stone-left-un-Rust-Oleumed approach. Slipped a repair kit — new piston, springs, and rubber washers — into the master cylinder. Stripped off the old brake lines and bought replacements, ramrod-straight new tubing with the screw fittings already in place on the ends. Brake lines curl and loop all over the place, and it didn't seem possible that I'd be able to bend the new lines to fit the intricacies of the chassis without collapsing tubing walls and springing leaks, but that turned out to be duck soup. Recoated the old backing plates with heat-resistant paint. Took the drums off to be lathe-turned back to roundness and smoothness ($3 per drum). Started reassembling. Once the parts are clean and in order, with replacements for what was worn or broken, it is more like manufacturing than repair work. I only had to pull the rear brake drums two more times (the $17 puller earned its keep) to put in pieces left out the first time around.

Ah, but see the way complexity creeps into the simplest of braking systems. Pickup trucks are by nature light in the ass end when unloaded. Most of them will lock up the rear wheels at the drop of a brake pedal on any surface offering less than perfect traction. Most pickup miles are driven lightly loaded. So braking power must be compensated between front and rear wheels. When a pickup is loaded, the weight bias is in the other direction and the compensation must be reversed.

I can imagine some mechanical-minded archaeologist someday picking through the bones of a 1950 Dodge pickup and re-creating the fiddling process that this weight bias caused. The rear drums are larger and wider than the fronts. The wheel cylinders for the rear shoes have larger pistons than for the fronts. Each rear drum has two single-action cylinders; each front a single dual-action cylinder. And so on. Imagine the engineering process. A single, solid, straightforward brake drum assembly is designed, manufactured, and affixed to each corner of the lowly Dodge. The braking performance is . . . terrible. Out come the slide rules; complex formulae involving hydraulic piston diameters and brake swept-areas are evoked. Pieces are changed. The braking that was terrible when the pickup was unloaded now becomes terrible when the pickup is heavily laden. More calculations, more new pieces.

This fiddling is before the fact, designed into the pieces that I am reassembling. There is not even much likelihood that I will mix them up, for they fit only in their proper place and the proper sequence. They represent only a glimmer of complexity to come: it is the clearest and most elementary aspect of automobile mechanics I can conceive, and before my very fingers I watch it grow into trigonometry, logarithms, technological necromancy.

There is more. A manual I have acquired spells out pages of detailed adjustments. The new brake shoes should, in fact, be ground to match the newly resurfaced drums — requiring, of course, exotic machine work. If not properly installed the shoes may wear more at the heel than at the toe, leading to grabby brake action. There are adjustments to align the shoes in roughly seven different directions and angles, micrometer adjustments, feeler-gauge adjustments, and to ignore any of them is to risk accelerated wear, poor performance, or early failure. Dire warnings sprinkle the manual's pages. There is the sin of reusing old return springs, the sin of mixing brake fluid types, the sin of improper bleeding of air bubbles from the system. Penances are left to the imagination. Trees? Bridge abutments?

Service manuals are hymnals of conservative thought. They are based on metal touching metal, what will go and what, absolutely, will not. They are not even pragmatic: there is never a hint of the "try this, then try this, and if that fails, try this" that is the operative method of real-world attempts to make machines survive. They are composed out of fear of failure and grudging acceptance of the inevitability of wear. Compensation for flaws, reaction to the destructive effect of actual use. Despair over the necessity, in an imperfect world, of having to recommend — ghastly concept — *tolerances.* Admissions of imperfection. The service manual posits the perfect machine, and tells how, when some dolt like myself has profaned that perfection through actual use, to restore it to perfection. Start with perfection, and then follow instructions. Precisely.

Screw it, I said, buttoning up my brakes. The truck was maybe months from running, and I wouldn't be able to test the effectiveness of the brake job until then. As long as it was sitting up there on the stands, wheels off the floor, no engine in it, every single one of those adjustments was just as perfect as those listed in the manual. As a stopped clock is right twice a day. Think about that, you manual writers with your .003s of an inch. It's all there, all new and/or shiny, all ready, and I will do my compensating and adjusting when the time comes to see if the truck will, in fact, stop. It's bound to have several hundred percent more braking than when I drove it into the barn.

Which left me with the feeling I used to get when I cheated on my homework. Slip it by the teacher somehow, maybe she won't read it and find out that I didn't really understand. Damn my service-manual head, with its niggling guilt over .003s of an inch, leaving me whirling between some metaphysical exactitude and what my bones tell me ought to work.

Screw it again. Scatter the coals, turn down the damper on the wood stove, go to the house. This was supposed to be fun.

As with brakes, so with steering. The steering wheel is like a big crank on a shaft that leads to a gearbox. The gearbox turns rotary motion on the shaft into linear motion, which moves a lever back and forth. That lever is "tied" to a rod (thus "tie-rod") leading to the right front wheel. One actually steers the right wheel, which "drags" the left along by means of a rod called the "drag-link."

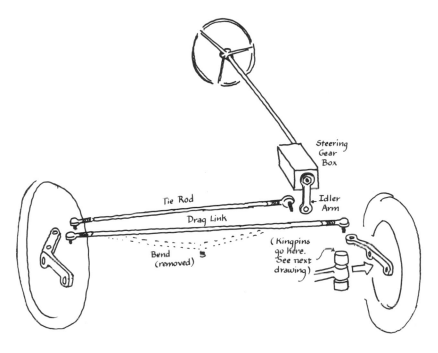

Dirt simple, but on my truck, most of it is shot through with wear and misalignment. The Dodge's drag-link runs parallel to and hides behind the solid front axle, but it droops a bit, and someone had run over a stump, putting about a ten-degree bend in the center of the rod, which in turn yanked the front wheels into a slew-footed stance. Elbow had remarked that he seemed to get only a few hundred miles from a set of front tires, and we'd chuckled together over the inexactitude of the steering.

So I pulled all of the above, cleaned it, examined it, and realized that I couldn't do much more than put it all back on again. I overhauled the steering gearbox, pounded the drag-link straight with a hammer (straight enough so when I rolled it across a concrete floor, it didn't hop up and down, which is not a guideline tolerance mentioned in a service manual). Replaced the tie-rod ends, repainted everything, put it back together. After walking around it for a couple of days, I set the toe-in of the front wheels at one eighth of an inch — by measuring on a stick with pencil marks from the center of the tire tread. This is also not how a local front-end alignment shop, with individual tire turntables, optical sighting devices, tool kits full of micrometers, would operate. (But I once saw a guy similarly "align" the front-end of a 180-mph race car.)

Here comes complexity again. Caster, camber, and toe-in (to make the vehicle track more truly and steer more easily). Ackerman effect (to compensate for the difference in arcs that the inside and outside wheels will have in a given turning radius). The minutiae that accommodate the forces generated by driving great weights at high speeds. Each wheel and tire becomes a large gyroscope at sixty mph; every vehicle must be controllable by the slimmest wisp of a driver. Have 5000 pounds of truck and load zipping seventy mph down the highway, and figure out how to keep the ride smooth, the steering effort light, the front wheels steerable and stoppable, the load stable, the direction sure and true, the maneuverability high. It is not so simple as gears and levers would have me believe, looking at that rudimentary steering system.

As it happened, that stick-and-pencil toe-in adjustment was about the only one available on the 1950 Dodge. Anything else was tied to the beam axle and the accuracy of its location. Go messing around with any of that and you start needing things like a press big enough to make adjustments by bending the axle itself.

Besides which, even to begin on any of that, I really had to remove the kingpins. Before I could start getting the slop out of the steering, or adjust the alignment accurately. Before I could be sure that at road speeds the front wheels wouldn't wobble and shimmy, before I could hope to have nice, smooth, secure braking. Worn kingpins are the source of most of the front-end troubles of the world. There's really no point in redoing either steering or brakes without making sure the kingpins are tight and unworn. And that being the case, there's no reason why

I shouldn't just go ahead and stick new ones in. They don't cost very much.

But to put in new kingpins, I have to remove the old bloody stinking rusted immovable ball-breaking kingpins. Yes. I simply have to get those old mothers out of there, one way or another. The question is, how?

CHAPTER 12

December, a Day

Late DECEMBER. Twenty-two below zero at 7:30 A.M. No new snow in ten days, and the seventy-five yards between house and barn is a crusted, discolored, ice-and-dog-shit wallow in the dark. Creak open the side door to the barn, feel with gloved hands for the light switch. Moving fast — not enough clothes on to loiter — I stuff some wadded newspapers into the wood stove, pile in three split birch logs, dump on half a cup of kerosene, open the damper, and light up. Swing the frozen bucket of soapy ice onto the stove and try to balance it there on its rounded bottom. (The bucket freezes first at the rim so its contents can't expand. Then it freezes solid throughout, and the pressure pushes out the bottom of the bucket into a perfect hemisphere. A little physics lesson that will cost me a perfectly good bucket by springtime.) Head back for the house and some coffee.

Should probably have chopped some kindling to have a more controllable fire during the day. Should have busted three or four more logs loose from the ice-covered pile I mistakenly stacked under the drip point of the barn eave last fall, so I'll have more firewood thawed and partially dried out for the rest of the day. Too cold. Give my little work nest two or three hours to get up to a bearable temperature, do all that later. Go languish over breakfast, screwing up my courage.

Ten A.M., most of the pot of coffee gurgling inside, the mail read and reread three times over, no putting it off any longer. Pull on several layers of clothing covered by grungy coveralls, boots, gloves for the first few minutes. Stump on out to the barn. The workshop proper, where the stove is, is up to fifty-five or sixty degrees, starting to release its accumulated stink of cold dead grease and petroleum solvents. The adjoining hallway where the truck sits — the open end temporarily sealed off with a flimsy fiberboard wall — is still frigid. I contemplate a rim of condensation ice on the differential hump. The wrenches I left on the barn floor threaten to stick to my fingers when I pick them up. It'll all even out and become bearable in another hour, after the stove is restoked. For now, it makes getting started character-building.

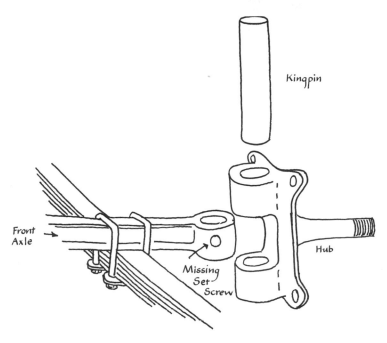

Today: kingpins. The kingpin is a machined solid billet of good steel, the hinge pin that allows the front wheels to be steered. It pins the yoke of the stub axle, on which the wheel is mounted, to the beam axle that bridges the chassis members between the front wheels. It is held in place by a set screw through the axle hub. To remove the kingpin, you unscrew the set screw and then drive the pin up out of the axle. The set screws are long gone on my truck, and the internals of the hub have rusted, freezing the kingpin in place.

I untangle the droplight cord, find a place to hang it under the left front fender so it lights the kingpin, and gather ball-peen hammer and drift — the latter merely a chunk of soft steel that I'll beat on to drive the kingpin out. I hunker down and, in the eight or ten inches of swinging room between the floor and the bottom of the kingpin, I give a tentative rap, staring hard at the visible top of the kingpin, looking for signs of movement. Adjust light, adjust working room, flap elbows once or twice, and whack it again. Nothing. I am on my knees, and I bend far over, checking to be sure I've set the drift against the kingpin and not against the hub. Whack! No. Whack whack whack, progressively harder. No. It is going to be one of those.

I try a whack or two on the top of the kingpin, on the theory that I might break the grip of the rust by starting the pin downward before driving it back upward. I can get a better swing in that direction. Nothing. Stop and think. Get a screwdriver and dig around in the hole where the set screw fell out about two million miles ago. The set screw that by its absence is making this job doubly or triply difficult. Go get a can of penetrating oil — I should have thought of this first — and squirt it in the set-screw hole, around the diameter of the pin, everywhere I can think of where the oil might penetrate into the hidden recesses where rust holds the kingpin in its death grip. Wipe the slippery oil off my hands, get hammer and drift, take a well-braced stance on my knees, give it another good whack, and get a shower of oil in the face, shaken off by the blow. No movement.

I decide to let the oil have a chance to penetrate a little better, give the kingpin another good soaking, and go to the house for more coffee. I bring the pot back with me and set it warming on the wood stove, while I idly stir the half-melted soapy ice in the steaming, teeter-tottering bucket. (Later I will be cleaning parts — I am always cleaning parts — and the soapy water, if it ever melts, will serve as a last washup before painting, to remove the kerosene.)

The assault on the kingpin enters its second stage, which consists of another round of whacking away with the hammer and drift — harder — and a resulting fine spray of penetrating oil all over me and the underside of the fender. Already filthy, what the hell, I just try to shield my eyes. More whacks — really bearing down, or rather up, now, getting some back into it, hitting hard enough so that the prospect of missing a swing and whacking myself is worrisome. No gain. Give it another dousing of oil and move on, let it steep.

Thus passes a long morning and early afternoon. A slug of oil, a few more whacks, no progress, let it sit, whack it again in a while. In between times I amuse myself scraping rust off the pile of removable floorboards stored in the back of the barn, taking each one as near to shiny bare metal as possible, cleaning it, painting it with red lead, and hanging it to dry. Every half-hour or so, more hammer work. Swinging the hammer stirs up a little body heat, and since I have let the stove die down and the barn cool off, it makes a welcome break to go beat on the kingpin every now and then. I recognize that I have another kingpin to get out once this one comes free, so I transfer my attention to the right front, with precisely the same effect as I'm having on the left. Thus I am now able to shift my attention back and forth, from kingpin to kingpin, leaving one to soak while I smash away, with rapidly shrinking patience, on the other. Without budging either the first millimeter.

I am into the seventh or thirteenth wave of assault — taking time out for a peanut butter sandwich and switching from coffee to beer, which doesn't reduce the frequency with which I have to step outside, fumble through several layers of clothing, and piss in the snow — when the light begins to go out of the day, heading for full dark by 4:30 P.M. A rouser of a day, all the way up to five above zero at two in the afternoon. I have paused to regroup, kingpin-wise, several times. I have thought of all I ever knew or heard rumored about kingpins, decided at least five times that I'm doing something basically wrong, rethought and reexamined the whole scene, dug through every service manual and how-to book I own, compared pictures and line drawings and exploded views. I am able to determine no other course than to keep soaking with oil and bashing away.

I also repeat every test I can think of to determine just how important it is to get the kingpins out. The stub axle swings smoothly and silently through its available arc, which means steering won't be affected if I leave the kingpins in. There is no detectable play in the camber angle. (Jacking up a front wheel, I grab it top and bottom to see if I can wiggle it. Sure sign of a bad kingpin. Mine are okay on that score.) There is only a very slight bit — maybe one sixty-fourth of an inch — of vertical play in the assembly. A tiny shim will fix it — but the kingpin has to come out so the shim can go in. That's the only reason I am removing the kingpins, to take out that sliver of vertical slop. That, and the nagging sense that if the truck is going to be made whole again, it ought to have new kingpins. That I ought to have done the job, to know . . . well, just to know.

I have also invented at least six inventions, using pulleys, levers, larger hammers, pullers, screw clamps, elaborate devices conceived to yank the old kingpin right out of there. All of them have failed to work. Finally, just about dark, I have a brainstorm. I need a constant source of pressure. I will use the truck itself. I have a small jack with a head smaller than the kingpin diameter. I place it underneath and jack up the truck so that the whole weight of that corner of the vehicle is resting on that kingpin: so that the jack is pushing the kingpin up out of the axle. Marvelously simple, sound, and clever. I give another shot of oil to the whole works and leave the truck in effect hanging by its left kingpin. Head for the house. With any luck at all, when I come back out the kingpin will have removed itself and the truck will have settled back down on the stands where it belongs.

Five-thirty P.M., zero degrees, windows all fogged up, cheery light beaming over the ravaged snow. Cooking smells, Chris humming around the kitchen, the pioneer housewife feeding her man. (I don't know if that's *her* fantasy, but it's the one I'll try to respond to.) I drop grease-encrusted coveralls outside the door, pad in on stocking feet, sluice off the first layer from my hands with industrial hand cleaner, scrub away at the next layer with household cleanser. Draw a bourbon, and subside, raw pink hands stinging, mouth watering, back muscles whimpering, into a soft chair. Flip on TV and almost doze before it gets warmed up. Harry Truman is hanging grimly on in the hospital in St. Louis, but he could go at any moment. I lose the rest of the newscast: two good swallows of the bourbon and I am dreaming of kingpins that slither in and out of their axle stubs like moray eels. Chris shakes me awake to eat, and getting up seems like a terrible imposition.

I'd like to claim that it was strength of character that drove me back out to the barn after dinner, but it was more like curiosity. I couldn't get my mind off my new brainstorm method with the jack, couldn't resist checking if with all that weight on it, the kingpin wouldn't pop right out. With the coals still smoldering in the stove, it was no problem to quickly heat the barn to a bearable temperature, and I was already filthy with grease and penetrating oil. What the hell, give it a couple more hours.

With the jack holding up the kingpin, I could now whack downward on the axle itself, which made for more effective whacking. A tap or two didn't do it. Another healthy dose of penetrating oil and a bigger hammer also didn't do it. The back of the ax head and an additional thirty-six inches of handle to swing with didn't do it. Nothing I could lift and swing would do the job, pounding down on that axle, trying to drive the kingpin out, trying just to *budge* the kingpin to prove that it was not an integral part of the steel of the axle. I finally ventured into terra incognita, lighting up the butane torch and heating the axle hubs to expand them, all the while trying to keep the metal of the kingpin cold, chilled down to minimum diameter. I don't like using heat, don't even like to fire up the torch in that oil-soaked barn of rotten wood (despite the fact that I keep flames licking heartily in the wood stove most of the time). I don't *know* about using heat to expand metal, don't know what it does to temper and hardness, how I might crystallize or warp or otherwise destroy good steel. I am not familiar with the colors of heated metal, with how one judges, visually, when it is hot enough.

But I am into desperation measures, and they force me to comical fumbling, juggling the torch and hammer and drift, long periods of just sitting, holding the torch on the axle yokes, listening to the sizzle of boiling penetrating oil working up out of the crevices. Shut off the torch quickly and set it out of harm's way and then get drift placed and hammer swung before everything cools off again. Burned fingers, muttering, yips of pain, disorganization, dropping of tools. Measured whacks. I am stifling the urge to fly into rage and whack-whack-whack, striving for meaningful blows, well aimed.

Nothing. I sit back on my heels and think, but what I think has little to do with removal of kingpins. The side door creaks open, and Chris peeks in, swaddled in my down parka.

"Hey, it's cozy in here. My God, you look worse than you did at dinner." I have the wood stove crackling, and with that and the torch, the barn is becoming saunaish. I realize that I am sweating; I've also spattered myself from head to foot with penetrating oil and wiped my face from time to time with a greasy coverall sleeve, and no doubt I am a trifle grubby.

"It's after eleven," Chris says. "I just thought I'd check to be sure nothing had fallen on you. I'm going to bed."

"Yeah. Well, I'm quitting. Be right in. I can't get the goddamn kingpins out."

"Did you know it's snowing? The temperature is coming up, and it's snowing hard. It's nearly ten above."

"Terrific." So that's why it is getting warm in here. "Well, . . . shit," I said, or words to that effect.

"Truman died."

"Oh, yeah?" I flinch at the not unexpected news, shooting a quick side glance at blue Dodge 1950 B–2–B short wheelbase pickup truck *The*

Harry S. Truman, kingpins intact. I resist a momentary flash of anthropomorphic fantasy. "Well, the poor old bastard, about time. What'd they say he was, eighty-two?"

"Eighty-eight," Chris answers.

"Eighty-eight. My God. Well. You go on ahead, I'll just pick up a bit and get the lights."

I coil light cords and toss tools at the toolbox, scatter the coals and damp the fire, shuffling in a three-quarter stoop against the ache in my back. Poor old Harry, finally gone, a generation past what seemed like a decent life span. Living on and on in God knows what state of tottering disability, shielded from the public embarrassment. Tough to the end, gum-jawed grit for weeks in the hospital. How tired he must have been when he finally let go.

As I was pounding on the kingpins. My head attempts to draw a metaphysical line between hammer on steel in northern New Hampshire and the gristly flutter of that dying old heart in a hospital in Missouri. And fails. Tries to mount a joyful Irish-wake mood over the merciful passing of dead old Harry Truman — sweet rest at last — and fails at that, too: when the ghost went out it didn't pass through Weston Valley, and there are no tremors in the air.

Just snow, and two knots in the muscle on either side of my spine four inches above my belt. No, what's in the air is calumny and vilification, heaped on the brown red heart of the rust holding those stinking kingpins frozen. Despite my efforts to put a sentimental twist on the end of the evening, I am full of spite and malice, at the set screws for falling out and allowing the rust in, at penetrating oil that won't penetrate far enough, at Elbow for faulty maintenance, at Dodge Motor Company for not providing some kind of snick-snack slide-fastener method of changing kingpins. At the barn that cramps my backswing and the winter that makes all this work slow and clumsy and, too often, painful. At the God damned truck. At myself, for my eternal blithering incompetence. I am tired, and my concern is utterly selfish; I can't support sweetness of thought even for the shade of Harry Truman.

I bolt the barn shut and stop on the concrete stoop at the side door for one last unbuttoned late-night piss in the snow. Exposing myself to the midnight woods. Sure enough, a couple of fluffy new inches decorate the doorstep. Fresh air on my face and soft, butterfly flakes that almost seem to sizzle when they hit the sweat. Channels of warm air pump up from my coveralls, playing on my neck. A reflective piss, followed by a little-boy shudder at the heat loss.

I will never get the kingpins out. The disassembled engine, back from the machine shop, rests in boxes, and I haven't even tried to put it together to see if the machine-work works. The new wiring harness sits coiled, a multiended snake evilly defying me to decipher where all those wires go. The cab is a gutted hull, empty sheet metal challenging me to turn it into a livable, drivable interior. The transmission accuses me from under the workbench — the exterior is cleaned, and I haven't had the courage to go a step further, to crack open that gearbox full of intricacies, for all my bold talk about rebuilding and totally understanding every part. The differential is still in the truck, wiped off, painted, and given a trusting pat, my little secret, fingers crossed that it will stay usable. My truck is now a barnful of tin cans full of nuts and bolts, and I will never, never get it back together. It will never run again; I have poured all these months and hundreds of dollars into sheer self-indulgence, big talk about defeating the technological monster. I am ending up with a barn full of junk — which is what I started with — and all for the dubious pleasures of the fantasy life I enjoyed while I was unscrewing all those nuts and bolts.

Or I will, finally, in my mad-inventor attempts to outsmart automotive physics, insert my lever in the one place that is absolutely, totally wrong, and bring it all down on me: truck, barn, wood stove, flames, solvents, gross tonnages, and mortal fire, pinned and burning — unerringly at a time when it is too cold to get the village fire truck started, which is what usually happens up here — and perish in my foolishness, just desserts for confronting the mystic entrails of the great god automotive.

Little-boy shudder indeed. Snow down my neck. I think I will take a long, hot bath and seek a supportive bosom. And put my truck toys away for a day or two. One can go crazy working on that truck in that barn all by himself all day.

CHAPTER 13

Management Mentality

CAREFULLY, carefully now, let us circle the great blue beast with the rust-colored tail. Do not let it get its bluff in. It was entirely too easy, I discovered in early winter, to take a couple of days off from this pleasant little hobby of truck reassembly and then find that the whole idea of going back out there — to grease stink and ice-rimmed tools — was just too utterly strange to think about.

It's easy enough to get inured to grease stink (a touch of brake fluid makes it almost aromatic), and wood heat can make the barn as cozy a place to work as anyplace a motor vehicle was ever permitted. Starting up was the problem. Inertia. To go out to the barn and begin work on the truck meant a certain fixed investment in time, else it wasn't worthwhile to get the fire going and the place warmed up. And once filthy — inevitably, instantaneously filthy — one did not quit work on the truck lightly. The cleanup was too laborious. Might as well stay and get dirtier.

The easy avoidance was to absorb myself in management. Administration. There were these several thousand parts to gather. Bearings, bushings, gaskets, hoses, seals, nuts, bolts, wires, clamps, braces, tubes, rods, levers, paints, lubricants, wheels, tires, springs, screws, washers. The planning job had to do with preparation of parts, subassemblies, assemblies, in sequence. Parts ready when it is time for the subassembly to go together, subassemblies assembled in preparation for the next step. Linear.

One can't do the rear brakes without the hub puller to remove the drums; one can't put the rear brakes back together lacking the gasket that seals the axle tube to prevent it from dripping grease into the brakes; one can't even — here it gets tricky — finish off the brake job by bleeding the brakes until the engine is back in, since the master cylinder bolts to the rear engine mount and gets in the way when one stabs that

900-pound engine into place, a job that is a delicate operation for all that weight. So why not leave the master cylinder off until later and keep all the maneuvering room possible? Except that means postponing the finish of the brake job, and if this linear progression continues one will never finish anything, and where does one start?

Add: the things you can't put together *right* until they are installed in place on the vehicle, in virtual ready-to-run fashion. The emergency brake mounts on the rear of the transmission. It has half a dozen arms and levers, a Rube Goldbergian affair that translates a yank on the handle in the cab into an external-contracting clamp in the drive shaft. I put those levers back together and mounted them on the transmission — in the ease and comfort of the workbench in the shop — the best way that my reason, spatial orientation, and memory told me how. When I remounted the transmission in the truck, every single one of them was bassackwards, which meant removal and reinstallation on my back, under the truck, working in darkness.

That is what my management skills were intended to avoid: the time when I couldn't yet do this because I didn't have that, which meant a trip to hardware store, auto parts store, or junkyard. Management should forestall all that running around. Elementary.

Out there in the real world of shade-tree mechanics (perfectly descriptive folk characterization, no matter how ill-suited to New Hampshire winters) and desperation transportation, the solution is always junk. It takes the place of management. Commercial garages carry extensive stocks on hand, and every serious-minded automotive repair enterprise has at least a few junkers stacked around the edges of the lot, ready to give up the minutiae of reassembly. The mechanics nevertheless run a virtual shuttle service to and from the auto parts store.

I dreamed of avoiding any more trips to the junkyards — now under two feet of snow — and the shuttle service as well, through sound management. Performed indoors, at the typewriter, with clean hands. I would outsmart the disorganized diversity of a zillion parts. Starting with the foolish dream of J. C. Whitney, Inc.

J. C. Whitney is this mail-order parts-and-accessories outfit in Chicago, which regularly cross-pollinates my mailbox with 160-page catalogues of finely printed pulp. Whole sections of parts for Model A Fords and World War II Jeeps. Obviously a prime source of exotica for

1950 Dodge pickups. I sat down with a catalogue and circled every item on every page that could possibly fit my truck (excluding Iron Cross replica air-cleaners, death's head gearshift knobs, and replacement gas pedals shaped like cartoons of bare feet). Went back through and composed a list of items I would, likely, actually need. Divided the list into sections based on the order in which, in a rational reassembly plan, I would need the parts. Fired off an initial order of $37.23. Waited.

J. C. Whitney runs somewhere between three and five weeks in delivery time, which elegantly complicates the prediction-and-planning portion of the managerial skills. J. C. Whitney did not in fact stock a large proportion of the parts I ordered, although their listings continued to appear in months to come in subsequent catalogues. And J. C. Whitney seemed to miss about as often as it hit in supplying parts for out-of-date Dodge trucks. Wrong parts. While continuing to toy with me with gaudy rubber stamps along the lines of "Reorder in 60 days," and "Back-ordered, to be shipped separately." Goodbye number one managerial dream; screw J. C. Whitney.

(The firm is, however, scrupulously honest in its mail-order dealings, if not in its product descriptions, and cheerfully accepts returns and refunds money. I've still got forty pounds of wrong parts in the barn that I haven't gotten around to returning, and have no doubt I'll get my money back.)

The auto parts store is reasonably good only on nonproprietary items. (If Dodge and Dodge alone made a part for the truck, the parts store will not have it; if anybody else ever made a replacement part for any item on the truck, the chances are reasonable that the parts store can locate it somewhere.) The local Dodge dealership had thrown away all its parts catalogues for pre–1960 vehicles. Sears, Roebuck would like to be in the mail-order parts business but doesn't stock much before the late 1950s.

That left junkyard snow-burrowing, or the nuts. There are a dozen or so magazines and newspapers for old-car nuts. They feature in their back pages advertisements for specific parts sources — specialized junkyards devoted to antiques, sometimes restricted to a specific make and a specific era. Few of them are interested in post-World War II vehicles, but there is an air of underground conspiracy among them, them-against-us-good-guys, and I decided to tap it.

I prepared a list of roughly a dozen parts I needed, beginning with the absolutely necessary, absolutely proprietary timing chain cover (the engine couldn't be replaced until I had it) and continuing down through such inconsequential luxuries as headlight rims and pedal pads. I ran off copies, enclosed the obligatory self-addressed stamped envelopes, and mailed my requirements off to the ten most substantial-looking ads.

Four came back stamped "addressee unknown." Three scrawled across the bottom of my list that they had no such parts. Two offered to supply a couple of the inconsequentials, at totally unreasonable prices. The tenth and remaining response offered me a timing chain cover for $5, made my winter, and left me half in love and damp-eyed over Armand T. Winship of Fontana, California:

DEAR MR. JEROME ;-

I see your in New Hampshire did you know the Mormons were there once. I am having trouble finding the parts list with the parts no.s in it but if it is a 1950 Dodge I know it when I see it and will pull the timing chain cover myself, $5.00 to you. Plus of course postage and shipping you'll have to pay that yourself, I'd like to trust you but people keep pushing me to far.

Ill get it in the next mail.

It is a small operation now, me and a Kid and of course Mrs. Winship, but when we were going "full blast" we would have as many as eight or 10 cars being torn down aday, totally catalogued and even partially cleanedup. We had a dipper vat then. You might not believe it but space is and always has been the problem even before Fontana got the "middle-age spread" and passed ordinances in restraint of our trade. Ten acres is all we have left, quess how many cars that will hold and Ill send you free a dimmer switch for your truck, no rust, out of the packing box, if you come with 20 of the correct number. We have a special technique for getting the most cars on the smallest lot, no its not on their sides.

I'd like to get into airplanes but they take up even more space and don't hold up in the outside storage, it rots thier fabric. I used to know the airplanes pretty well from watching them at Randolph Field in Texas, "The West Point of the Air." I was not at Randolph but over at Ft. Sam Houston, a buck sergeant, and could see them fly over and go on Sundays to see them parked. Would you believe a shavetail Lieut. named Dwight David Eisenhower used to borrow 10 bucks from me now and then for the post poker game. He was a lousy poker player and I never voted for him knowing that. I think he still owes me money, from his grave that'd be. Ryans, PT-something, some number, maybe 14, were the planes. The PT stood for Primary Trainer. They killed a lot of fine young men in them, which they also did in the war, of course.

I don't have no help for you on the rust, it is always the problem. We deal in parts and not the work, ha ha, that's the hard part I always say altho busting some of these fenders off is not childsplay. Door glass we got, plenty altho it may be for a 1949. For running boards, consider plank fabrications?

Glad to see someone keeping the old trucks running, they have been the lifeblood and backbone of this country, those folks who say its the railroads haven't been out to see whats going on in 40 yrs. And I always preferred to have a steering wheel in my hands. I really beleive in trucking as an industry and would put my money in it if I had any. I had little truck experience myself but drove crosscountry in a 36 Plymouth in 1940 just before the War, a sweet running little car if you didn't try to push it in the desert. Everyone had those canvas waterbags on thier bumpers so the evaporation would keep it cool. We didn't and like to died, it felt like. I asked a man in a filling station for a little taste from his canvas bag, and it was cool for a fact.

Well, I ramble on, always glad to have a new customer for our little business, it keeps us going some but we dont mind, it is something to do. I will turn 75 next May 1, May Day but I always say Im no Communist, it was my birthday before it was thiers. Mrs. Winship is even older but she does not like me saying it. It could be that our partslist Book is around here somewhere but I am almost sure that that young man who took the Oldsmobile parts just pinched it, he was awfully interested. You can't keep them out and you can't check everyone of them when he goes out, it would be like going through a mans pockets.

However I trust you Mr. Jerome and am forwarding that timing chain cover as soon as I get it off, please remit $5.00 on receipt and postage and insurance, you can tell what it was from the sticker on the package.

Some of our parts are mint, some we call perfect used, but we don't let anything go out we would not put on our own pride and joy. It is a 1940 BUICK with fender-mounted spare, Franklin Roosevelt used to ride in one, a real classic and I keep it running like a watch. And not an Ingersoll, either. No offense to the Ingersoll people, they try hard.

Goo luck, Mr. Jerome, on your own project, and you let me know those other parts numbers. You expressed interest in. Parts numbers always help and I expect my partsList will turn up one of these days it always seems to, then I can look them up. If I don't have the part I may have the advice, so just try me. Will mail to give you time to think about it, regards to Mrs. Jerome if there is one, Armand T. Winship.

CHEERFUL REGARDS;
ARMAND T. WINSHIP.

I sent the $5 plus enough to cover postage and insurance; the timing chain cover arrived two months later, air-mail special delivery. God knows where he had to go to dig it up.

CHAPTER 14

In Search of Ground Zero

GET EVERYTHING CLEAN. Try to get it right the first time, as constant disassembly and reassembly increases the possibility of ruined parts, stripped threads. Make sure there is a lock washer under every nut and a washer under every bolt head. (Lock washers can be eliminated where there are double nuts.) Keep small assemblies together, in the proper order of reinstallation until time to reinstall them. Get everything clean again before it goes on. Take apart the small assemblies, clean them, put them back together immediately before forgetting their order. Work methodically through small assemblies, adding them to larger assemblies. Before the large assemblies become too heavy, bolt them into place on the truck, avoiding future hernias. Paint everything first, so hidden surfaces are at least partially protected against rust.

Periodically empty the random tubs and vats full of solvents and small parts, and break down the small parts into loose categories. It is a worthwhile exercise to acquire several dozen old coffee cans, and sort into them the nuts, bolts, washers, and lock washers. It is even a reasonable step to further divide the nuts and bolts according to fine- or coarse-thread types. Another can will fill up quickly with springs, another with brass fittings, and several with otherwise uncategorizable pieces, most of them fairly intricate little metal stampings that make absolutely no sense until the moment comes when just that shape, and no other, will solve some exquisite small mechanical problem.

Get everything clean.

Welcome, in other words, to the obsessive-compulsive world of reassembly. The idée fixe is simply to fit parts together smoothly, to be able to bolt them up. Place the nuts on the bolts, turn the screws, pull everything nice and tight, done. Yes. Tab A in slot B, cereal-box premiums, Dad on Christmas Eve figuring out how to bring the new toys to the working stage. If they came apart, they will go back together. Sure.

The investment of time in the reassembly process does not go to putting nuts on bolts and turning screws. Two percent of the reassembly time is so satisfyingly spent. Ninety-eight percent of the time goes to staring. No, ninety-five percent to staring, and the rest to fetching.

Staring is hard to explain. Much of it takes place at the truck proper, when one is faced with a small subassembly that has, for example, four mounting bolts, and one finds that the place where they belong, where you distinctly recall removing them *from* two months ago, has only three mounting holes. At that point you hunker back, find some place to rest your weight, and stare. You will be turning the piece in question in your hands, and also in your mind, mentally trying it this way and that, attempting to imagine other ways it could possibly fit, and I suppose this activity could be classified as some form of thinking. But mostly it is just staring. The mind fogs over. One struggles to snap it back to attention to the problem at hand, but it does not snap. It is not that the mind drifts away to sunnier climes or pleasanter pastimes. It doesn't go anywhere. It just stops.

More commonly — most commonly of all — the staring is aimed at that collection of small parts. Twenty-four tin cans full of nuts and bolts, and nowhere among them the single tiny metal item necessary to proceed to the next step. I flash on a mental picture of the kindly old workman with grizzled face, a gnarled finger poking nuts and bolts about in the cans as he searches for that essential nut. Humming, perhaps, or some gentle tuneless whistling: world enough and time, good-humored patience underlying the search. In fact there is no whistling; what you hear is keening, whining. The picturesque old workman actually has to go to the john — parts searches affect you that way, automatically — and besides, what underlies the search is really not patience but despair. The necessary nut isn't there. It is a common, ordinary nut, and while there are 276 of those in the collected cans, none is the right size. And if the right one doesn't turn up, most of the day's work will be lost as you put aside, clean up, make a trip to town, etc. No, of course you don't make a trip to town for a single nut. Yes, of course you make a note of the need, put aside that particular assembly, and move on to something else. And pursue it up to the point of *its* missing nut, and slide off to yet another point of attack, with a growing sense that the truck will soon consist of nothing but dangling, incomplete assemblies, each with its own essential missing nut, bolt, washer, pin.

The missing nut *is* never found. There are two-dozen cans filled with small parts from the truck, but none of them belong. None of them can be used for anything. How can all these pieces come off but not go back on, not fit anything anymore, be totally useless? It is one of the things you ask yourself during your staring.

You save them anyway. You always save all the small parts that you have no use for. Everyone always saves all the small parts. My house is 140 years old, and every single one of the string of ten or fifteen owners has always saved all the small parts. There are antique berrying baskets in the shed, piled full of antique small parts, none of them any longer identifiable, none of them ever conceivably useful for anything. When it is time to face any hardware-oriented household task, I go to the shed and stare at my 140-year-old accumulation of small parts. Poke around in the containers. Keen softly under my breath, as my bladder fills. Knowing the small part I need is not there.

Dreams develop out of this experience. Most householders eventually dream of owning a hardware store. I want to rebuild my truck *inside* an auto parts store, browsing the neatly numbered and boxed bins, plucking what I need, extemporizing. Concocting new connections, inventing solutions to the requirements of seal, joint, clamp, fastening. I'd happily pay for what I needed, shiny-new off the shelf, still saving money by avoiding extra trips. The frustration is standing on the other side of the counter, trying to predict needs and describing them in terms the clerk can comprehend, so he can browse for me. (Thus the hardware store, where I have browsing privileges, is better for standard small parts than the rigidly un-self-service auto parts shop.)

Dither, dither, nuts and bolts, small parts and tiny decisions. There is no way to make the fitting of a new washer challenging; stripped threads are not heroic. One merely replaces the bits, however one has to do it, because it would be stupid to do anything else. Anything else is cheating. Cheaters' trucks break.

The subassemblies do accumulate, and grow into larger and larger assemblies, bolted up tight, finished-looking. As one adds them onto the truck, a new phase begins: adjustment. It is no longer a matter of simply cinching up tight. Now one must place parts into relationships, into the midrange of mechanical possibility. And, somehow, secure them halfway between no-contact and unworkable metal-to-metal.

As in the clutch. The clutch is simple enough in principle. It is a purely mechanical device that clamps the crankshaft of the engine to the drive shaft of the rear wheels by way of the transmission. There is one smooth disc of steel on the crankshaft, another on the main shaft of the transmission, and sandwiched between them a layer of the corky brake-lining material to provide the friction to stop them from slipping. When the clutch pedal is depressed, springs force the two discs apart, and engine and transmission are disconnected. When the pedal is let out, springs force the discs together to compress the clutch lining between them so they can't slip, and the engine drives the transmission. Which, if it is in gear, drives the drive shaft, which drives the rear wheels, which drive the truck.

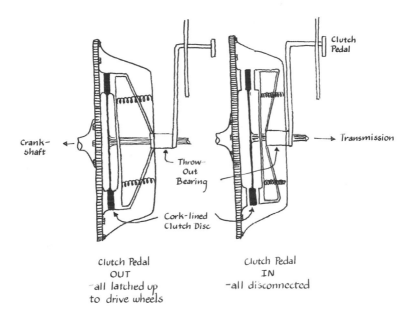

Clutch Pedal
OUT
—all latched up
to drive wheels

Clutch Pedal
IN
—all disconnected

I disassembled, cleaned, and examined my clutch. The linings seemed fine, nice and fat to take up eventual wear, neither glazed nor oil-soaked to allow slippage. I reassembled it, overleaping book warnings about elaborate dial-indicator measurements necessary for perfect alignment of the discs. I put it back in the truck, bolted back neatly in place, clean and shiny. And found I'd lost ground zero in the process. I needed to adjust the clutch, and I really couldn't do that unless the truck was running. There was no way to get the truck running without an adjusted clutch. I felt like I'd lost the point to mount my Archimedean lever, whereby to move the world.

On the face of it, it is not so complex. Clutches are adjustable to allow for wear. The adjustment must be made so that when the pedal is out, the discs clamp together with enough pressure to contain the driving force of the engine without slipping; and when the pedal is in, the discs are far enough apart so they don't touch, which would make them heat up and glaze the lining.

At one end of the adjustment range, the clutch would in effect keep on driving whether the pedal was in or out. At the other end of the range, everything in the clutch would be totally disengaged, whether the pedal was in or out. It certainly seemed that one should be able to find a workable point between those two extremes. And to find it within the range of movement of the clutch pedal and its assorted levers, some of which are also adjustable. One ought to be able to figure that out.

But lying on the floor upside-down, head of me to tail of truck, reaching up into the no-longer exposed innards and working by feel, attempting to reconceive hidden directions of movement involving a series of arms and levers that reduce a foot of movement at the clutch pedal to three quarters of an inch of movement at the clutch plate — via several reverses and ninety-degree bends and bell cranks — I grew confused. I began musing. I projected ahead that I would be similarly cast adrift, with no shove-off point, in locating the camshaft in its 360 degrees of possibilities. In installing the distributor. In trying to reachieve carburetion with a totally rebuilt carburetor, every possible adjustment screwed down tight. In plumbing the mysteries of electricity as I scrambled to rewire the bloody truck.

There on my back on the creeper, with maybe eighteen inches of elbow room and a good crack on the head waiting in any direction I moved, I began to feel lost in space. In my tightly insulated little box stall in the barn, wood stove pumping my sweat out of the breathable air. No starting point. Flat on my back, legs spread, my good ole 1950 Dodge looming above me, I began to get fucked by doubt.

"Ground zero" is poor terminology; the space metaphor is more apt. I recalled the moon shots, with the astronauts sitting in orbit, picking their point in space and time to fling themselves a quarter of a million miles toward where, if the computer hadn't also gotten fucked by doubt, the moon would be, three days from the moment of flinging. Could a computer locate my clutch plate for me? "Say, Mr. Programmer, I have this nineteen fifty Dodge B-2-B half-ton short wheelbase pickup truck (got to give them all the numbers) that I took apart too far. I have lost my way and . . ." I would say. "Garbage in, garbage out," he would respond, the ultimate tag line, computerdom's vaudeville joke.

I did a short stint in "aero-space," as we called it, a decade ago. They provided all the numbers, 103-foot Titans, 9000 gallons of fuel burned in the first 3.0 seconds, hypergolic reactions and all that. They told us about celestial navigation, secret stuff. (Celestial navigation? Holy electrical engineering? Divine business administration?) The missile silo had a quartz crystal window on the sky, yards away from the concrete hole itself, and a vacuum-sealed tube leading down to the computers in the bowels. That way the star fixes by which they aim the missiles would not be distorted by temperature variations between ground level and the computer room, or by microscopic flaws in imperfect plate glass in the sighting window.

They also informed us about a perfect tracking system someone had devised for space shots. A straight line is drawn due west from ground zero of the launch site, and another due south. Then, 1000 yards from the launch site (exactly), radio equipment is set up. Ten thousand yards from ground zero (exactly) more tracking equipment is installed. And again at 100,000 yards. From this, one achieves perfect tracking. They tried it in Florida, and it failed. Florida moves around too much. It might have worked in New Hampshire granite, but Florida is built on shifting sands. I guess to hit what you aim at, you have to know where you're at when you throw.

Then I got off into some foolish speculation about driving a stake through the heart of my truck and thus nailing it to the garage floor — "There, by God, *located!*" — and starting from there. Nonsense. I knocked off, awaiting an idea to deal with my clutch.

Precisely aimed from a micrometrically calibrated launch pad at Vandenberg, an intercontinental ballistic missile is fired 6000 miles "down-range" (fortuitous vagueness) into the Pacific. From an atoll in the Pacific an antiballistic missile sees; hears; senses approach; fires;

flies a hundred miles above the earth's atmosphere; finds its target. They meet. Our toys work! Scientific jubilation. Now: let's devise an even **harder** *task.*

I went with a village father to the green, to help his children launch model rockets. Three successful firings of "conventional" toys, and boredom sets in. Double-charge engines (higher). A larger tube (heavier). Double- and triple-staging (more complex, longer in time). All the possible permutations on the equipment, then boredom again. Finally, inevitably, a mouse and a clear plastic tube, with tiny airholes and a miniature parachute. And, of course, a misfire, and a casualty callously accepted by these nine-year-old technicians. All predictable (scientifically). They brought the mouse along in the first place, didn't they?

The hot line is periodically checked by transmitting over it translations of poetry — in code. It must be checked because it is not in constant use, Moscow and Washington having nothing, ordinarily, to say to each other. Disuse deteriorates (technical failure is possible), and the means of communication must be kept open. There may be something to say. Art is coopted to fill the breach. Transmutation achieved, epic into currency, sonnets into wafers of exchange, zipped along the wires, spat out at the Kremlin, translated. Decoded? Examined? Merely checked against the authorized text?

"What does it say?"

"It says the hot line works." Decoding is difficult: poets are not trustworthy in their use of language.

Meanwhile we are perfecting that other means of communication. Wonder of the world: twin parabolas launched without prior discourse. **They** *meet; they* **speak.**

CHAPTER 15

Supercold

DEEP WINTER NOW. Heavy winter. The world a rock-hard frozen solemnity, the top six feet of earth a solid sheet of diamond-chip high Rockwell ultrapermanence. The ground frozen so solid that the concrete highways ripple like silk, new frost heaves shoving humps into the roadways overnight. (Old frost heaves newly reappeared, rather. The same ones come back in the same places every year. It is dependable: after January 15, I have to slow down just before the bridge over the creek beyond Colby's barn.) The earth groans and strains at this expanding skin of ice and literally spits up granite boulders. Thus the pastures do in fact grow rocks, and in the spring farmers must get out and stone them, adding to the fences that surround the fields.

I don't care how many times I've experienced it, how long I've been here, what preparations I've made this year, in my head or in my house. When the hard cold hits, there is an element of fear.

Big storms are easy. Too much snow fills me with wonder, makes me shake my head, disoriented, and leads me out to commit unnecessary silliness, digging through drifts, getting vehicles stuck, stepping off solid ground into crotch-deep immobility. In fact the big snowstorms bring everybody out — the snowplows never stop — and for all the howling bluster of the storm, there is a kind of background noise of human activity, almost happy. It is good for the confidence to be continually reminded that all those other folks are in the same fix.

That's all stifled by supercold. When the storm blows out, the wind stops, the sky clears, and the massive shudder of ultracold air drifts silently down from Canada and hammers us into the house. Clear air and thin sun at three in the afternoon, and maybe five above; a twenty-five-degree drop by five-thirty, pitch dark, twenty below, and fifteen more hours of sunless black downward momentum to the thermometer before the first hope of relief. It is too quiet out there.

Plenty of wonderment in this situation, too, and we always bundle up
at least once to go out and . . . try it. The first inhalation builds a tiny ice
rim inside both nostrils; the second intake hurts. I wander for a few
minutes before the cold penetrates my clothing, step away from the
microclimate surrounding the house — a few dozen feet away, as if to
make sure I am really *outside*. Then I stop, breathing lightly, and simply
try to experience. Listening. Too bloody quiet, entirely too quiet. Only
the extra-sharp squeak of footsteps in below-zero snow, and then — wait
for it — cannon fire off in the woods, as some foolishly juicy tree
explodes, frozen sap expanding to shatter a limb. *Crack!* Scary. Trot
back to the house.

God *damn*, get the lights on, put on some music, draw a hot bath, let's
get some action going, let's sustain life here. Batten down, cover up,
crank up the furnace, throw another log on, heat and light. Keep moving,
dance and sing and chafe the hands, caper a bit, have a drink, toast the
cold, applaud nature's showmanship in laying on this impressive
demonstration.

Then settle down, hyperactivity subsiding, gathered in the glow of
light and heat, repeating to each other, yes, we are cozy, yes, we are safe,
and the record runs down, the fire turns to coals, quiet again. Distant
crack of another shattered tree, loud enough to raise the hair on the back
of my neck. Once or twice during the evening a great shuddering groan
or a crashing thud from the old timbers of the house as it warps in the
wrench of frozen foundations and supercooled air. I get up and check the
thermometer again, always, every time it does that. My God. Another
five degrees, and not midnight yet. Try to imagine the hour before dawn,
outdoors. Beasts alive, out in that night.

In the really bad spells, the supercold arrives on such a night, sinks its
teeth in, stays. After twenty-four hours or so — long enough to leach off
any pockets of remaining warmth — we get high thin overcast and a
brittle wind, which simply continue; the weather is no longer
phenomenal, it does not sustain wonder. There is no longer a fluty feeling
of shock and awe at this powerful display of antiheat put on by the
weather systems. There is just enervating, leaden, depressing cold, day
after day, ten below at high noon, thirty below at night. One hangs alive
from strings of fuel oil, electricity, water, preserving the continuity of
the supply with care, very aware of that external dependency.

Supplies run out. On New Year's Day we needed milk and bread, and I faced up to starting the car, trying to make the world work again. The block heater was on the blink, but I had brought the battery indoors the night before to keep it warm and it had sufficient cranking strength to get me going. (Years before, after one forty-five-below-zero night, I reinstalled a warm battery, jumped in the car, and it started right up — but the plastic seat cover shattered when I sat down on it.)

Twenty below at 2:00 P.M. on a holiday, in search of bread and milk. The car shudders and groans long after the engine is warmed up, the shock absorbers frozen, the tires almost square from frozen flat spots, the road a milky white salt-dusted washerboard of frost heaves. Every gear a groan of anguish, the heater blower squealing on dry bearings as it blows pallid air to frost over the inside of the windshield. The car tells me, clearly and distinctly, that it is an imposition to be moved on such a day.

Such a day: gray sky, hint of piss yellow sun, swirling wind picking thin spume off last week's snowdrifts. Town is boarded up for the holiday, nothing open. Once moving, I refuse to give up, and try the next village, and the next, a forty-mile round trip on a rapidly fading day. Nothing. I am short of gas and can't find even an open filling station, which is legitimately frightening. No cars move, no faces show. What blows across the road is equal parts salt, ice crystals, and tattered paper scrap. Or ghosts of dead bears, for all I know, and I panic, heading home, milk-and-breadless and low on gas, to hide. Wait it out. They have to get it moving again sometime.

They do, of course. Less than halfway through a six- or eight-day cold snap, everyone grows as impatient as I am and begins coping. Life resumes; once one has the vehicles working and commerce restarted, once one adjusts, compensates, then it is just a cold snap. The change in mental attitude is this: at the beginning of a cold snap, I figure if the furnace fails during the night I will simply die, my frozen bones to be discovered in the spring. By the middle of a cold snap, when things are going again, I realize that if the furnace fails in the night what will really happen is that the pipes will freeze and I'll have to redo the plumbing.

The transition — from worries about mortality to worries about cost — is something I don't want to ponder during a cold snap.

I didn't get much work done on my truck during the supercold. I did rebuild the carburetor in the house one night when things were too fearsomely unpleasant out in the barn. Carburetors are fun: hundreds of tiny parts, gaskets, little brass nozzles and valves, and no appreciable internal wear. So rebuilding is simply a case of taking everything apart, getting it extra-clean and back together again — with several adjustments to check in the bargain. An idealized and miniaturized version of what goes on with the whole truck. An orgy of anal-compulsive nit-picking, thousands of grooves and channels of cheap pot-metal casting to rout out and scour clean. Understand it? It is only an old-fashioned Flit gun, a perfume atomizer, hyper-undersimplified by technological progress into a seat of mystery. Mostly, though, during supercold I left things alone, the truck out there brooding on its stands in the barn. Stayed in, banked the fires, waited. Another snowstorm would be along eventually, low pressure to the northeast, swirling warmer moist air from the sunny southlands of lower New Hampshire and northern Connecticut, the classic pattern. Up twenty degrees on the thermometer, and another six inches of calendar-art fluffiness to cover the ice-ridge and salt-waste harshness of the cold spell. Wake up to still air, bright sun, new snow, heaven's great cheerful sigh of relief. Whistle up the dog, grab cap and jacket, saunter forth, hands in pocket. Saved again.

There's a half-mile loop of connecting roads near my house that's almost always plowed for comfortable walking, and almost always totally deserted. I can walk around that after a new snowfall, in fifteen-degree weather, on January 5, and if there's sun shining and not too much wind, it feels like spring. Especially if the dog goes along.

CHAPTER 16

The Lost 180 Degrees

A FRAGMENT of film from the early 1950s has lodged forever in my head. In *An American in Paris*, Gene Kelly awakes in a tiny Parisian garret and proceeds, in a dream of fluid motion, to perform his morning ablutions. Everything in his tiny warren folds, stows, collapses, becomes something else. He totters groggily, yawning and scratching, and with rump, knee, elbow, and head he rebuilds sleeping space into living space without an unnecessary glance or a wasted motion. Simultaneously he kicks his Murphy bed into the wall behind while he pulls down a folding breakfast table with one hand and fetches clothing from an overhead line with the other. It is a dance, and a parody of dance, and a demonstration of the niggling tyranny of physical objects somehow totally controlled.

I used to trade with a cashier/short-order cook at the takeout window of a coffee shop in New York who was better at this than Gene Kelly and Hollywood. He filled the morning orders instantly: coffee (light, dark, or regular), bagels (cream cheese or butter), Danishes, toast, tea, milk, hot chocolate, whatever — slap dash bang and into containers, lids sealed, sugar packets, wooden spoons, straws, napkins, money taken, change slapped down, *next!* He was sour-tempered and almost evil, but Jesus, he was fast. One steeled oneself before stepping up to that counter, rehearsing under one's breath the briefest and most economical phrasing for one's order. Quickest cup of coffee in town, and strangely enough the coffee was very good.

Not exactly all deliberate speed: *hysterical* speed. All necessary objects readily at hand, location and condition known, logical order of progression. No wasted motion. Dream of mechanical rationality.

It occurred to me during my management days, readying subassemblies and lining up parts, that my whole idea was really to assemble the world's largest erector set. A truck kit, spread out over the barn, so that all I had to do was put things in place and run up a bolt here and there. Foolish dream. The closest I came to realizing it was with the engine, for which I got the most outside help. The machine shop did put together an engine kit for me: a block, a crankshaft, and a box of parts.

The block was sound, freshly bored out to a larger cylinder size to accommodate wear and remove the ridges. That meant all new pistons (supplied) in the next larger size. Valve seats honed, and all necessary replacement valves furnished. Amazingly, the old crankshaft proved good: straight (its bearing surfaces in alignment) and round (the bearing surfaces had no flat spots and thus didn't need to be reground). A fly cut had been taken off the cylinder head to insure its perfect flatness. A sound and healthy engine, just waiting to be snapped together.

The scene is the dingy floor of what used to be the milking stalls of the barn, on a winter night. Cheery fire in the wood stove. Despite the way I have festooned the place with lights, I work in a murky glow, relying mostly on a rubber-covered sixty-watt droplight that I can hang inches above the work in question. The engine block rests on 4 x 4s on the floor, where I can strong-arm it to any useful position (until it gains too much weight, as I add pieces). A pile of clean rags, a squirt can of oil, rolls of paper towels for wiping parts, nearby boxes and cans of small parts, gaskets, gasket sealer.

I am lost in a dream of 1950s technology, craftsman at work, parts that fit, no stripped threads, rust banished. The droplight makes a warm cone of focused attention, the remainder of the barn dissolving into darkness. I neatly oil and wipe every machined surface, preparing for the mating of metal to metal. It is virtually the only time that winter's fantasy of methodical mechanical tinkering is fulfilled.

Piston ring end-gaps measured, filed square, slipped onto pistons. Pistons fitted to rods, the wrist pins an easy push-fit. Rods fed down into cylinder bores, piston rings compressed, pistons slid gently into prelubricated cylinders: maximum sexuality. Cam followers, which have been soaking for months in light lubricant with number tags affixed, are now slipped back into their original guides. Camshaft fed oh so gingerly lobe-by-lobe into the new cam bearings, installed in the block by the machine shop. Prenumbered valves, already hand-lapped, slipped into their valve guides, the springs and keepers snapped into place.

Except for bolting on the cylinder head, the top end of the engine assembly is done. Elapsed time: maybe an hour and a half, after a month of walking around that box of engine parts, afraid to tackle the job of doping it all out. I am, of course, cookbooking it together, following a manual paragraph by paragraph. Pause to rotate the camshaft, just to watch. Cam lobes raise cam followers, pushing on valve stems, opening and closing valves, a working valve train completely assembled and doing its job nicely, just like the book says. I built that. I put all those pieces in there, and they seem to work. Clever 300-pound toy.

Gaining weight by the moment. (As I gain momentum, excited by this clean, clear assemble-ability.) I bolt the head temporarily in place so I can turn the engine on its back to work on the bottom end. Fit new bearing shells into the upper half of the main bearing webs — little pot-metal semicircles that make all the difference in how long the engine will live, once it is running again. I horse about ninety pounds of shiny clean crankshaft into place, setting it down gently, gently now into the new bearing halves. Laying baby in the cold steel manger. Done. New rod bearing half-shells into the rods, and the rods pulled up into place against the crank journals. All the bearing caps laid out in a row, four large mains and six little rods, and new bearing shells fitted to them. A half-inch of Plastigage laid on each bearing journal, caps laid over, rod nuts and main bearing nuts spun into place. All twenty nuts torqued down to the specified foot-poundage, then removed to check the bearing gaps.

Plastigage is a commercial product, a tiny, hairlike strand of colored plastic that expands, when crushed, at a controlled rate. I lay a wisp of it on each journal, between crankshaft and bearing shell, and tighten the bearing cap. When I remove the cap, all that remains is a colored stripe on the bearing surface. I compare that stripe with printed stripes on the Plastigage package: too wide a stripe of crushed plastic means the bearing is too tight and vice versa. Ingenious. To tighten the cap to the proper pressure, I use a torque wrench (Sears, $11.87, useful elsewhere) to measure how tight I am twisting the bolts, in foot-pounds of torque. Doubly ingenious. Thirty minutes to bolt up the bottom end.

Except that everything has to come unbolted to check the Plastigage readings, and then — everything on the mark, the measuring and machine work performed by the Techno-Kings turning out to be reassuringly accurate — I leave it undone and approach the problem of setting the cam timing.

Turning the cam for the pleasure of watching the valves move up and down indicates that the valves are mechanically timed to work in the proper relationship to one another. But they are not, as yet, related to the piston movements. For the engine to run, the valves must open and close at precise intervals in relation to the progress of the pistons in the cylinders. Cam timing.

There is a gear on the front of the camshaft, connected by chain with a gear on the front of the crankshaft. There is a dot inscribed on the cam gear, adjacent to the valley between two gear teeth. There is another dot inscribed on the crank gear, adjacent to one of the teeth that lines up with the cam gear valley. In the best of all possible worlds, one lines up the two dots as the timing chain goes on, and the cam is then properly timed. Nothing could be simpler.

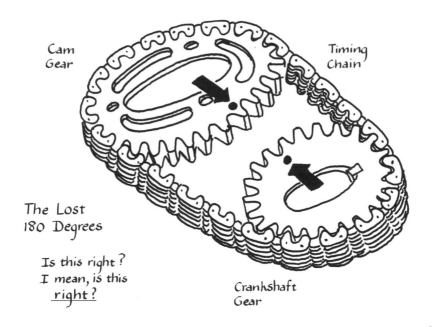

Cam Gear

Timing Chain

The Lost 180 Degrees

Is this right? I mean, is this right?

Crankshaft Gear

But. The cam turns at half the speed of the crank, and it is also possible to get the two dots to match up perfectly when the camshaft is 180 degrees out of phase, in which case the engine will not — cannot — run. This is the essential shade-tree mechanic's idiocy, the original sin of engine jobs, the standing joke, the error most likely to creep into reassembly. Particularly when cookbooking an engine together, when simply by following the instructions and matching the two dots and then buttoning up the rest of the engine, one has a fifty-fifty chance of being totally wrong, no matter what the cookbook says.

The depressing part is that I will finish assembling the engine and hoist it into the truck and bolt it down and figure out and attach all the electrics and fuel supply and radiator and accompanying hoses and transmission and clutch and all that, and then try to start the engine before discovering whether the cam is right or wrong. And then if wrong, I'll have to remove the radiator and transmission and clutch et cetera and get the engine out and tear it all the way back down so I can pull off the timing chain, rotate the camshaft 180 degrees, and then put it all back together again. This is wasted motion. To avoid this wasted motion, I must understand valve timing. It is humanly impossible to understand valve timing.

This is why it is humanly impossible to understand it. For the valve timing to be correct, both intake and exhaust valves for the number one cylinder must be closed when the number one piston is at top dead center of its power stroke. Said number one piston *also* comes to top dead center during its exhaust stroke, and it is difficult to tell exhaust stroke from power stroke until the cam timing is correct. This leaves me in the position of being unable to get the cam timing correct until the cam timing is correct, or I'm in search of ground zero once again. Actually, if I pay any attention to the exhaust stroke at all, in the matter of cam timing, I'm dead — which is difficult when I can't tell which is the exhaust stroke.

The procedure is further confused by the fact that the number six piston is located on the same crankshaft plane as cylinder number one (but 180 degrees out of phase, of course), so number six is approaching top dead center every time number one is doing the same. If I pay any attention to piston number six, I'm also dead, but it is happening, back there at the back of the engine while I'm trying to concentrate on number one, and it's hard to ignore. Particularly if I get to thinking that when number six is on the exhaust stroke, number one is on the power stroke, and so if I could determine which stroke six is on, I could then dope out number one.

This is all so self-evident to experienced mechanics that the manual doesn't bother to tell me much about it. It merely tells me that for the valve timing to be correct, both-intake-and-exhaust-valves-for-the-number-one-cylinder-must-be-closed-as-the-number-one-piston-is-at-top-dead-center-of-its-power-stroke. And then leaves me to wander off into the gauziest sort of philosophical speculation.

The manual also neglects to tell me which way the crankshaft rotates when the engine is running. This is even more self-evident than the discrimination between exhaust and power strokes. But when I have the engine upside-down and backwards at my feet, and in bare-block form, all reference points like distributor and fan removed, three months since I saw the bloody thing running and no real confidence anymore that there is even any international standard or customary usage that applies, then an even more whimsical sort of speculation sets in.

Staring, as in small-parts searches. Long hours of staring. Vague rotating motions of the hands. Penciled diagrams on the barn wall. Turnings of the crankshaft, observation of the positions of valves and pistons. Jotted notes, followed by more crankshaft turnings, followed by more notes. It is all there, the pieces connected (wrongly or rightly) so that they move each other, all linked to transmit motion, nothing missing. A large iron puzzle. Nothing mystical or abstract or intangible, perfectly linear. Pure logic will work it out, and when the solution is found it will all fit, the relationships so orderly that it will seem impossible for those pieces to be assembled in any other way.

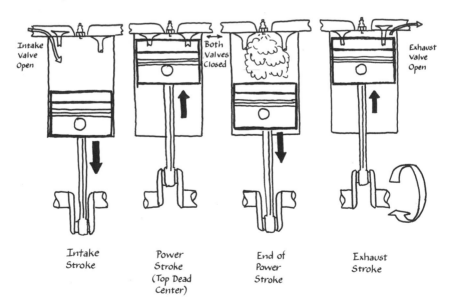

(As the piston sweeps down the intake valve opens, and the rapidly increasing vacuum sucks sweet, cool fuel mixture to fill the space. The piston pauses momentarily at bottom dead center, the intake valve closed to seal the last leak. Upward the piston drives, compressing and heating its load of gases, shrinking the combustible space. Spark fires, gas burns, at the momentary apogee. The piston is driven down by the burning explosion. Another pause, the exhaust valve begins opening to vent the burnt gases, the piston sweeps up again to clear the cylinder of waste. Pause. And down it goes, intake open again, swirl of new fuel, the cycle repeats. Pure linearity.)

In my knot-tailed youth I was a high diver, a trampolinist, taking every opportunity to fling myself into the air, from almost anything, to see what didos I could cut while airborne and still arrange myself for a painless landing. I toured one summer with a traveling water show, as a clown diver, one of several semiprofessional high-altitude fools. Folk wisdom among our crew had it that if you started a stunt correctly and kept on going, you were all right, but don't hesitate. There was a phenomenon that regularly overtook us which we described simply as "getting lost." It happened to me once in every two or three evenings of performance. I would make my customary approach on the diving board, straining for height on the hurdle step, riding the spring of the board through its maximum pitch, and then hurtle upward into space — and get lost.

It was probably no more than spatial disorientation from some break in the rhythm, a slick surface on the foot mat on the board, a momentary failure of concentration. Lost. No way to get it back, to recover any sense of where I was or how I was moving. Once the linear progression through whichever flips and twists was interrupted, all sense of how to continue flew out of my head. I no longer could even tell up from down. There is nothing for a diver to do in such a situation but collapse into the tightest possible ball — to present as little surface area as one can manage to the coming impact with the water — and prepare for pain. It wasn't even funny as a piece of showbiz, those crippled, collapsing flights.

Having gotten my head lost in the orderly progression of establishing the relationship between piston and valve, I packed it in at midnight and went off to bed, stunned. Visions of opening valves and ascending and descending pistons whirling behind my eyes, and never any way to link them solidly in time. Fever dreams.

The next day I called Ray, a mechanic friend who I presumed would be immune to confusing speculation.

"Well," said Ray, "you match up the mark on the cam and the mark on the gear when pistons one and six are top dead center."

"Right," I said, scribbling furiously.

"Then you turn the crank one hundred and eighty degrees."

"Right."

"Then you turn it *another* hundred and eighty degrees, and if your cam is right, the exhaust valve on number one will open."

"Oh, right, of course," I said, still writing.

"If it's the intake that opens, you're a hundred and eighty degrees off."

"Gotcha."

"When it's right, when the exhaust valve on number one opens, the intake valve on number six opens too."

"Okay."

"And when it's wrong, the intake on number one opens, and so does the exhaust on number six."

"Wait, wait," I said, "I don't think you'd better tell me anymore."

"Gee," said Ray, "I hope I said that right."

I ran for the barn with my notes. I'd left the engine with pistons one and six sitting at top dead center the night before. I turned the crank 180 degrees, paused, then started on the second 180. Exhaust on number one began opening. Right. It was right all along. "Nail it," I muttered to myself, and began cinching down main bearing bolts, finishing up the bottom end of the engine. Everything put back in order, all neatly done according to spec. Then I turned the crank through a couple more revolutions, checking every ninety degrees or so with Ray's notes. Right. Still right. Has to be right.

Gee, I hope he said that right.

After that it was just kit building, timing chain and precious new timing chain cover, seals and tubes, oil pump, water pump, gasket gunk, nuts and bolts. Leaving off the angular, bulky components until later, for a lighter and more manageable package to hoist and stab into the engine bay. I wrestled the assembled engine back into the central stall of the barn, where the truck stood waiting for it, and called Chris. Bolted a chain to two corner head bolts and fastened the hoist to the chain.

Chris worked the hoist — nervously — while I — nervously — guided that monster engine, once again approaching its original weight, up over the front end of the truck and down into the engine well. Nervously indeed, both of us almost dancing about the task, afraid of all that weight and the soundness of hoist and chain and barn rafter. Ready to dart out of reach at the first unusual groan. It held. We settled the engine down onto the engine mounts. Bolted it into place.

In again. The slim, bare-bones, unaccessoried old flathead six once again resided in the truck where it belonged. We hadn't dropped it on ourselves or the chassis; the scary part was over. It had gone like silk, not only the engine replacement but also the major part of the engine assembly. Except for the cam timing nonsense.

And the oil pan. I have to admit that it took me an hour or so just to put the pan on. All it is is this big roasting-tin affair, an oversized tin can that functions merely as an oil reservoir and a cover for the bottom end of the engine to keep road trash out of the crankshaft. But it has a low spot and a high spot, and I had this vision of what the assembled engine was supposed to look like, and no matter how I tried, the pan kept fouling on oil pickup lines and wouldn't go on right. I moved and readjusted and redesigned oil lines for an hour before I realized that my vision was 180 degrees backwards, and I was trying to put on the pan back to front. Embarrassing. Once you get lost, there's just no getting it back until next time.

CHAPTER 17

Black Magnetism

START WITH an engine turning 3000 revolutions per minute, which is a reasonable highway speed. That means the crankshaft is turning over at fifty revolutions per second, so each piston is making fifty strokes per second. Half of these are power strokes, and half are exhaust strokes. For the power strokes to do their job in keeping the engine running, there has to be a spark at the sparkplug at just the right instant of each of the twenty-five power strokes per second that each of the six pistons makes.

That means that in an old flathead six there are 300 piston movements per second, and the ignition system has to send a discrete, high-intensity spark to every *other* one of them. Not just randomly to every other one, of course; the ignition system must in effect select which of the six pistons that is coming up on its turn for a little shot of fire. Look here, ignition system, there are these six big holes — cylinders — in the block, and in each one of them a piston is bobbing up and down at fifty times a second, and what we want you to do is hit each one of them on the head with lightning every other time it comes to the top. Got it? Once you get the rhythm, it'll be a snap. But you're going to have to be faster than Buddy Rich.

If I could get so lost in the middle of the linear regularity of the valve train, imagine what terrors ignition promised. There is some hope of understanding things that work with levers and fulcrums and ramps, and even things involved in the flow of gases, like carburetors and exhaust systems. But electricity is all mumbo jumbo, black magic. Mystical nonsense. The lady who worried about electrons running out of the empty wall receptacle and piling up on the living room rug had a point. They have been trying to tell me for years that electrons can be introduced into one end of a perfectly solid copper wire — not a tube, mind you — and they will flow through that solid wire and come out the other end. Sure, I say, right. And toads make warts.

The only indication that the ignition works is that the engine runs. Or you can pull a plug wire and actually see the spark jump. Or you can ground the wire with your hand and receive some of those lightning hits that were supposed to go to the top of a piston. Plug another system into the ignition system, so the lightning shunts away from the sparkplug and goes flesh-arm-nerve-spine-zap, and you leap, offended, and snap back your hand.

There are three "separate" electrical systems in an automobile. There is the starting system (ignition switch, starter, battery), the charging system (ignition switch, voltage regulator, generator or alternator, battery), and the ignition system (ignition switch, coil, condenser, distributor, sparkplug leads, sparkplugs, and battery). Actually there is a fourth system — everything else, which includes the lights, instruments, and accessories. It is perfectly characteristic of the sinuous vaguenesses of electricity that all of these systems use each other's wires, dip in and out of each other's circuits, refuse to be sequestered into rational separate entities.

Faced with this kind of flagrant deception, I cheated like crazy on my vow to understand my truck. I bought a new battery, voltage regulator, ignition switch, coil, condenser, distributor rotor, points, distributor cap, sparkplugs, and leads. And I allowed The Wire King to build me a complete new wiring harness, stem to stern, for a mere three quarters of the price of the original used truck. Madness.

The greasy old wiring harness was returned to me bearing number tags on wire ends, along with a fine, new wiring harness — really gorgeous workmanship — with duplicate numbers. By laying the old harness alongside the truck and making rough estimates of where the old wires had fastened, and comparing them with the similarly laid-out new harness, I began to identify circuits and to hook up the new wiring. With what is for me a burst of electronic ingenuity, I fashioned a lantern battery, a flashlight bulb, wire, and alligator clips into a device for checking continuity. With that and a wiring diagram, duck soup. Or at most a soluble puzzle, an eighteen-foot conundrum. Start with the short wires on the wiring diagram; find the wire in the harness, by length, number tag, and continuity; hook up both ends, as, for example, ignition switch to ammeter; go to the next longer wire. Every wire identified and fastened in place reduces the number of remaining mysteries. When I finished, everything worked except the fuel gauge, which didn't work when I bought the truck.

"Think of it as water," a friend had said, cryptically, when I moaned about the vagueness of electricity. Right. So the power source — the battery — is the top of the mountain, and ground, no matter where it is physically located, is downhill. The bottom of the valley. Okay, I can handle that. A switch is a dam, and when it is thrown the sluice opens. So far, so good; build an irrigation system, carrying rivulets of little electron bullets to everything electrical. No, not *to* everything electrical; *by* everything electrical, since the electrons must be taken up again, in another canal, on the other side. A canal that leads to the bottom of the valley. The metaphor works. The generator is a pump shoving the electrons back up to the top of the hill.

I can hook up a circuit that way, but I'm not a millimeter closer to understanding. I have replaced the electrical system in my truck, and I don't understand ammeters, fuel gauges, voltage regulators, coils, condensers, starters, generators, or turn signals. Or why, according to the metaphor, when a wire is too small for its current it heats up (friction, resistance, Ohms) instead of puddling the extra electricity into a pile on the way in. They tell me that if I whirl a magnet inside a coil of wire it *makes* electricity (generator), but if I put electricity through a coil of wire inside which is a lump of iron, it turns the iron into a magnet, and if I do it just right it whirls that magnet and acts as a motor (starter). Why is this? Do I believe in stuff like that? They tell me that if I dump a sheet of lead into a tub of acid, that makes electricity too. Sure. Drop that toad, Willy, before we have to take you to Oral Roberts. What's an ampere-hour, Mother?

A friend of mine, a professional pilot, once ran a small charter operation with rented aircraft, and I met him one day as he was memorizing the preflight checklist for an unfamiliar plane. He would stare off into space, his eyes glazed over, and mumble through the items: "Gear locked, flaps down, magneto on," whatever. Then check himself on a printed card. It sounded a bit like a liturgical chant, and I began to imagine that it was. The pilot taxis the plane to the end of the runway and says this prayer list of items, then essays a takeoff. If he has enough faith, the airplane flies. Every once in a while there's a loss of faith.

There's a lot of that in aviation. They hook a bunch of ceramic lumps together with copper wires, place them in a dome on the top of the airplane, run electricity through them, and then sit down inside to watch a glass plate with moving dots of lights behind it, and they think that keeps them from hitting mountains and other airplanes. Faith. Usually works.

(Let us not even speak of the Defense Department, which digs 103-foot holes in the ground and installs monster totem poles in them. Totem poles with more ceramic chips and copper wires in them, and hollow insides pumped full of exotic chemicals. And they think these totem poles keep us safe from Russians and Chinese. Who have totem poles of their own.)

When I cookbooked the engine together, for all my confusion, I could still understand why each step was called for. It was all laid out, made good sense; it was perfectly obvious that within the cast-iron parameters of that engine it was necessary to have this or that clearance, adequate tightness here and looseness there, an order of progression that enabled all the parts to work together without getting in each other's way.

I cookbooked the electrics together too, but I didn't know baked Alaska from split-bean soup. All I know is that I hooked the wires to where the book said they should be hooked. And everything (but the fuel gauge) seemed to work when I was finished.

I succumbed to the black-box method after all, for all my railing against it. I pulled the black boxes from the truck, the boxes which might or might not have worked (in fact were working when the teardown started) but in which I had lost faith. I went to the auto parts store, dipped a knee as I crossed the threshold, fluttered a hand through the five points of the Chrysler Corporation penta-star emblem (adopted long after my Dodge was manufactured), and stepped up to the counter to profess my faith. Bought new black boxes, more blessed by the gods than the old. Those old black boxes probably had demons in them by now anyway.

CHAPTER 18

Realities

IT TOOK ABOUT six months to wire the truck. In between hooking up the first wire and hooking up the last, half a year. It wouldn't be fair to overlook that.

It all started one evening in late February when I had just finished tearing three starter motors completely apart in hopes of building one that worked. One starter came from the truck, another from a box of parts that Elbow threw into the deal, and the third from a junkyard, $1. I scattered them all, picked the best bearings and best brushes from the bunch, cleaned everything up, reassembled a single starter, painted it a nice forest green, and turned to contemplate the three generators stacked before me, destined for the same process.

Three grungy, grease-caked generators, one of which, when I first tore into the truck, was still in quasi-working condition. Trouble was, I no longer knew which one it was. Or what, if anything, was wrong with the other two. Or why. It was just at that point that it flashed across my brain, as if on instruction from the ghost of Gottlieb Daimler: "I don't want to do this anymore." I stood up, walked out, latched the barn door. Enough.

I would go inside, take a hot bath, put on some soft clothes, sip a bourbon, and think about it all for a while. Chris, elegantly sympathetic, concurred: "You ought to leave it alone for a few days, the way you've been going at it." Yes. I would take a break.

Then I had to go make money for a while, and it was March and then April, and before long the garden had to be started, and the creek had warmed up, and any number of high-priority items had to be addressed before I could return to the truck. The money situation was only moderately — i.e., customarily — desperate. Along about there I heard from a wealthy acquaintance who, interested in my truck, told me about his own. It was in California, being . . . done. People out there can rebuild anything, do infinitely superior work to the original, turning rusted heaps into mint-clean remanufactured motor vehicles in every way more precisely assembled and beautifully finished than anything any automobile factory ever turned out. For a price. Ship boxes of parts to Los Angeles, followed by boxes of money.

Lord, if I had that kind of money, I could spend the rest of my truck-project time fingering paint samples and comparing upholstery fabrics. Um, yes — fly out to the Coast in a few months and drive back a brand-new 1950 Dodge pickup truck, a charming little trifle to use around the estate. No way. Not interested. But I thought about those guys out there a lot, the expertise, the facilities, the total inconsequence to them of what were heroic tasks to me. Like stabbing the engine back into the truck. Or hooking up wires.

Cost-no-object wasn't what I had in mind, but I had still poured nearly a thousand bucks into my inoperative $200 truck. Ridiculous. Most of it in two horrifying chunks, $250 for the engine machine work and $150 for the wiring harness, which sum total could have bought me instead two more barely operative trucks. And then, as with the starters and generators, I could've taken the three apart in hopes of putting back together one good one . . .

Okay, but I never intended to do it all out of bailing wire and old coffee cans. If my approach was (gigglingly, semiseriously) Thoreauvian, I never intended to build a $24 truck and then live in it for two years. Hang the extravagance for engine work; without it I would never have had a chance to plumb valve timing. And if the wiring harness was simply a failure of courage in the face of all those fishy electrons, it was also a great timesaver, allowing me to have my truck back together and earning its keep by the time I walked out, latched the barn, and went to the house for some clean clothes. Nothing wrong with *that* kind of planning.

Making money meant traveling, reporting, coming home to write. Usually it didn't interrupt things too seriously — a few days out in the field, then home with a suitcase full of notes, and I could write mornings and work on the truck afternoons and evenings. And almost keep us within sight of a shaky solvency. (Particularly with Chris's help; she did the same sort of work from time to time.) Nice life: fire up the wood stove in the morning to warm the barn, and go back inside to pound the typewriter until noon or so, when my brain began to fuzz over. Then exchange words and paper for nuts and bolts, and a little decidedly nonmental therapy. (More nonmental than it should have been, perhaps, which may have been part of the problem.) Any psychiatrist's prescription for maintaining mental health, right?

Then why did mine get so strange? I will not pussyfoot around delicate psychological states: after that night in February when starters and generators lodged in my craw, I could no longer go back to that barn. Or I could, but only to shuffle tools around for half an hour, sweep the floor, rearrange the work space, and come back in. My writing went well, and my head would turn to mush right on schedule in the early afternoon, but I couldn't handle the other part of it. I could not face my fucking truck.

I found other things to do. Spring arrived on schedule, the house got painted, the garden went in nicely. We had lots of visitors, fine times down at the creek, trips to Texas and Ottawa, diversions without number. A glorious summer — hot, fairly dry for New Hampshire, full of activity. Even the bugs laid off early. I would like to report that I took up the clarinet or glass blowing or something, but I did not. Mostly what I did was not work on the truck.

Do not sell short the advantages of having a single repository of guilt. Everything that was wrong with that summer — *everything* — sat in the barn, a dank, blue, $1000 reproach. The fanciful dream of, my God, now *two* winters ago, slowly reacquiring the rust that I had so patiently scraped off and painted over. Sitting there, sullenly accusing me. Want to walk up to those falls on the backside of the mountain? Take the bikes and go hit tennis balls? Hitchhike to Ecuador? Be with you in a sec. Anything to hide from that presence in the barn. A perfectly glorious summer.

On August 12 I had owned the machine for one full year, and hadn't really touched it for most of five months. This nonsense had to stop, and I began stoking up my child-of-the-thirties guilt for another sustained run at it. Gritted teeth.

I had long ago torn down the flimsy wall that kept the work space winter-cozy. I proposed now to push the truck out of doors, to work on it in summer sunshine — part of my despair obviously produced by the winter's worth of soot, ash, and cloying smoke-filled funk. The truck was still on stands. (Watch it. We *know* about getting it down off the stands now, okay?) Before putting it onto its own four wheels, it only made sense to finish off the brake job that had been 95 percent completed the previous November. Just adjust the shoes one final time, then bleed the air out of the system; I'd only put it off because it took two sets of hands, and a helper hadn't happened along at a handy time.

With a practically nude engine block in place and no inner fenders, there was plenty of room to stand inside the engine compartment, where I could most easily get at the front brakes. So I climbed down inside the right front wheel well, tightened the brake shoes firm against the drum, then backed them away just out of contact, like the book said. I climbed back up on the fender to go around to the other side, jumped lightly to the barn floor, and broke my foot in two places.

Still trying to kill me. Oh, I laughed all the way (as I crawled) to the house: that malevolent blue bastard sitting out there, plotting. The Revenge of the Machine. Ingenious adversary, Inspector; I had really thought it would yet find a way to drop an engine on me, and all the while it had this other devious scheme saved up. Intellectual jujitsu: one uses the opponent's stupidity, rather than his weight, to throw him. All it had to do was wait me out, of course.

Too bad there's not a cellar beneath that floor so I could crawl back, torch the barn, and have Milton Louderback come over with his bulldozer to push the charred remains into the hole. It's what they always do, up here, with buildings that have outlived their usefulness. Buildings no one plans to enter ever again. A good load of topsoil, a couple of pickup loads of horseshit, and we could plant a healthy corn patch where the barn used to be. The Harry S. Truman Memorial Corn Patch. If I only had a truck to haul the horseshit with.

Well, maybe not quite like that. A little foolish talk while the bones knit. I thought I would be able to work on the truck with the walking cast, but I couldn't. I could hobble back and forth to the creek, and even immerse most of me while there. I could ride a bike. Somehow I just couldn't twist wrenches with a cast on my foot. Tells more about the health of my head than my foot.

That took care of August and most of September and was probably a good thing: the inactivity festered to the point that I would do anything; hell, I'd even work on the truck if I could regain full mobility. Mid-September frosts flattened the garden, and I worked some of the soreness from my newly liberated foot uprooting the fence, due to be replaced next spring. God's little object lesson, getting in the last tomatoes, cleaning up the dead garden — if I didn't haul ass on the truck I would either have to rebuild the false wall in the barn or work in a wind tunnel through the coming winter.

I hauled ass. Ordered plywood and insulation for the wall, musing on how I could carry it home myself and save time and delivery charges, if I only had a working truck. Then we got this reverse curve of Indian summer, and I stacked the materials to one side and plunged ahead with the truck, secretly swearing that I'd have it outside and running before the wall needed to be built. The foliage turned color, New Hampshire filled up with tourists, the house processed its usual string of unusual visitors; I ignored all, buried in the truck. Leaves fell, people left, weather held, truck kept right on going together. Stiffness left my foot. My hands, softened by a summer of dithering, cracked, cut, scabbed over, healed, and finally toughened up again enough to support a sustained effort. I'd forgotten about that — how sore my hands were when I first started work on the truck, how long it took to get them in shape to work. Weather kept holding, and I put off rebuilding the wall.

Anyway, that's why it took six months to get the wiring in the truck. If I could learn from episodes like that, I'd probably draw some neat moral lesson about pacing myself, not going at it too hard, avoiding a certain tendency to taunt myself with wildly optimistic and totally artificial schedules. Obviously that's not the way I learn my lessons. I tried several psychological stimulants during that gorgeous summer. Motivation: I really *needed* a truck, there were piles of scrap all over the place, things getting out of hand, stuff I'd been putting off for a year because some day I would have a truck to do them with. Economics: that thousand bucks tied up in old and new parts, so few of them bolted to each other, all that money I had so many better uses for. Reward: if I get the goddamn thing running, I will drive it to Southern California and lie on the beach for a decade or two. If I get the goddamn thing running I will not have to work on it when the temperature is twenty below zero. If I get the goddamn thing running I will give myself a present and never touch a wrench again as long as I live. Challenge, or maybe humiliation: Herb Whitethaw, down at the corner, can figure out how to assemble a motor vehicle, and he's so dumb that the other day when a burning match head caught under his thumbnail, he put his thumb on the sidewalk and *stomped* on it to put out the fire.

None of these reasons worked, or all of them did; I somehow just rolled back into it, working at a pace that fluttered away at the underside of panic. And the truck did start going together. Amazing. This wire seemed to belong here, which meant that wire went there, and all those little black lines on the wiring diagram began to describe a comprehensive system that made sense.

Finally I ran out of wires. The engine stood in the engine bay in spare elegance, without carburetion, exhaust system, cooling system, oil filter, most of the necessary works. Wouldn't hurt to turn it over a time or two, as it had been reassembled with plenty of oil. I placed the hot new battery into the rusted-out old battery box and hooked it up. Checked everything I could think of one more time. Climbed into the driver's seat and turned on the ignition. The 1950 Dodge was built before the days of starter solenoids. The starter was activated by pushing a spring-loaded mechanical foot lever. My foot delicately on the starter button, I probably genuflected somewhere inside my head and shoved it home. Groan. Groan. Groan-groan-groan-groan-groan.

Son of a bitch. That sounded like an engine trying to start. It gave me the very strange feeling that the good truck *The Harry S. Truman* might some day run again. That was really scary.

CHAPTER 19

The Other 180 Degrees

REALLY ROLLING NOW. All the bits and pieces removed from the engine so long ago have to be put back on. Another Chinese puzzle, plugging all the holes in the engine block with the proper appliances. A stroke of absolute blind luck: another 1950 Dodge truck turned up in the area — well, 1952, close enough — and for three weeks I regularly flagged it down, lifted the hood, and stared desperately at the engine, trying to memorize just where everything belonged. The owner understood — he'd gone through much the same process years before.

Exhaust and intake manifold, carburetor, fuel lines. Header pipe and muffler. Oil filter and assorted lines, tubes, filler caps. Shift linkage and blind-stab-guesswork clutch adjustment. Radiator and hoses, and fourteen hose clamps left over. Et cetera. It reminded me of hanging ornaments on a Christmas tree. Finally it began to look like a truck engine, except that it was suspiciously clean.

And finally a day came when I began having trouble finding anything else to *do* to the damned thing, to get it ready to run. Then a bit more luck: Strell happened by, in the middle of a rainstorm. He was driving a recently acquired '63 Chevy flat-bed truck that had suffered a total collapse of the windshield-wiper system. He needed a warm, dry place to work and some tools. I needed him and his truck.

Strell is roughly five feet tall and two feet wide, gnomish, sort of a cloud of intense, fuzzy black hair with clothes on it and two bright eyes peering out. There was room in the front of the barn for his truck, and we spent a few companionable hours on our respective vehicles, taking turns with the droplight and handing each other tools now and then.

"I was about to come looking for you guys," I said. "I'm just about ready to try to get this thing started, and I'm going to need a tow."

"Whatsamatterstarterneedatow?" Strell seemed to be asking. Actually he was responding right along with me, in conversational style, but Strell talks in a soft voice, at exactly the same volume whether you are standing next to his mouth or in the next room running a chain saw, and at about 200 miles an hour. It takes a while to establish much give and flow to the discourse.

"Well, the starter works," I said, "but the engine's too tight. All new bearings and everything. It needs to be towed a bit to get things working, get gas up to the fuel pump and all."

"Oh," said Strell, loosely translated. "Bruce has got a *big* truck now. Four-wheel drive. He could tow you good."

"That'd be great. Is he still staying up at Susan's?"

"Yeah. But the truck isn't there," Strell said. "It's in Concord. Something's broken. It isn't running."

Terrific. A certain amount of indirection here, I noticed. "I was going to ask Sepp to do it — he's got a truck, and he really knows what he's doing with engines."

"Jimmie's got a truck," said Strell, standing beside his new truck. "When are you going to be ready to do it?"

"Next day or so."

"Boy, old Loose Bruce could tow you good. It's really a big truck. Powerful, you know?"

I had to leave then, while Strell stayed to rebuild his windshield wipers four or five more times. The next morning I was back on the truck and pretty well wrapped it up: no point in putting any more of it together until I had it running, or found out I needed to tear into it again. I made a trip to town for one last recharge on the truck battery and to drop in on Strell & Company. I found Loose Bruce.

Bruce is the stylish member of the group, usually sporting a rakish hat decorated with porcupine quills, sometimes at least partially clean-shaven. Jimmie looks like a wistful twelve-year-old, with the saddest eyes — like a medieval icon, Chris says — but is the experienced subsistence farmer, perhaps even the master craftsman of the group. I think they were intrigued with my project — they'd known the truck when it belonged to Elbow — and had been richly entertained by my compulsive parts-cleaning, my outrageous expenditures, my broken foot, the whole thing. They were doing a little pickup carpentering in town, laying up cash against the winter, but they weren't minding shop. I found Loose Bruce at the health food store, eating raw groats or something.

"Hey, John, got your truck ready to go," Bruce said. Perfect New England reading — a question uttered as a statement, no question mark at the end. Bruce is from New Jersey, I think.

"Yeah, I think so. I'm looking for someone to give me a tow."

"What happened to Strell?"

"He said we ought to use your truck, if only it wasn't broken . . ."

"Naw, we'll do it with Strell's truck. When do you want to do it?"

"I'm not sure Strell wants to. How about Jimmie's truck?"

"Naw, we'll do it with Strell's. When do you want us to come out?"

"I thought maybe I'd find Sepp — he knows a lot about . . ."

"Naw, we'll do it with Strell's. We'll come out at lunchtime tomorrow."

"Okay." Okay okay okay. Jeez, Strell, you can't say I didn't try.

Home, then, to map out the campaign. The truck was bare chassis from the cab back, minus hood and lights. All the plumbing and electrics were, I hoped, in place, and a few precious gallons of gas in the tank. All driving controls and instruments in, and some of the floorboards installed. I'd neatly bolted the off-breed seat to the floor to eliminate the wobble. Ready. Couldn't think of anything else to do.

The next day I lucked into a drizzly, thirty-five-degree day — lucky for a November 20 in New Hampshire, lucky to be above freezing. The battery had stayed in the warm kitchen overnight, along with the crankcase oil. I stoked the wood stove in the barn to a roaring fire to raise the ambient temperature of truck and engine block. The closer they were to operating temperature, the better the chance that the truck might operate. At noon, I carried buckets of hot water from the house to fill the block and radiator. By the time the crew showed up in Strell's truck, I was reduced to dancing from one foot to the other, wiping the windshield and checking the oil level for the twelfth time.

"You got a chain?" asked Bruce.

"Yep." We hooked the two trucks in tandem, with ten feet of slack.

"You got any brakes?" asked Jimmie. Strell winced.

"Gee I hope so. I went through them completely."

"What's the plan?" asked Bruce.

"Let's go around the loop, stay off the state roads," I said. The loop started opposite my driveway. "Get me up on the flat, and I'll ease out on the clutch a bit and turn it over a few times. Then when we get to the top of the hill, stop and we'll unhitch. I'll wait until I'm coasting down the hill to try to start it. That way I won't have to worry about bumping you while I'm fiddling with it."

"Boy," said Strell, "if we had that four-wheel drive we could *really* pull you around."

We started out, Strell's unladen flat-bed kicking up gravel in the driveway, spinning its wheels to get us in motion. Jimmie swayed on the truck bed where he could watch the action. The old blue Dodge jerked reluctantly into motion for the first time in fifteen months. The right rear brake was making hideous scraping noises. The steering felt nearly as bad as before I overhauled it. The shock absorbers and springs, unweighted by the lack of a bed on the rear, pitched me all over the cab. The driver's sun visor kept flopping down into my face, forcing me to hunch over the steering wheel to see. It was a *terrible* truck.

Up a slight hill, onto a level stretch, and test number one. I put the clutch in, shifted to what I hoped was second gear, and let out the clutch to see if that worked after my eyeball clutch adjustment. A lurch, a bit of a slide, and slurping noises from the open engine compartment indicated that, indeed, the engine was turning over. Those shiny new engine internals could now begin learning to work with each other.

Test number two, because I couldn't wait. I turned on the ignition and fed a little gas. Not much happened. And then, low whuffing noises, and several large blue white smoke rings came belching out of the carburetor.

Shit.

Cam was off. One hundred and eighty degrees off. Had to be. Engine was so mistimed that what fuel reached the sparkplugs was getting burned while the valves were still open and then popping back through the carburetor.

We coasted to a stop at the top of the hill. Everybody got out to confer. We unhooked the chain. "I'll go ahead and try it on the hill," I told them, "but I think I already know what I needed to find out. I turned it on back there, and it didn't do anything but blow smoke out the carburetor. I think the cam's a hundred and eighty degrees off."

"How did you do that?" Loose Bruce asked, unloosely.

"Shit, I don't know. I figured it every way I could."

"You can go crazy trying to figure out valves," Jimmie said.

"Yeah. I *did*. I even called Ray when I was halfway into them, to get him to tell me how to dope it out."

"Should've called Sepp," Bruce said.

"Yeah." They pushed me off. The truck and I creaked and fluttered down the hill. Pop, pop, more smoke from the carburetor. Nothing else. No hint of power pulling us forward; only the dead sensation of riding momentum against compression, gravity rapidly running out. The hill was long enough to try it two or three times, in second and third gear. Nothing. I lurched to a stop against compression. They picked me up, rehooked the chain, and towed me back to the house. We unhitched and rolled the truck backwards down the driveway to the barn.

Conference in the driveway. "Valves are a bitch." Yeah, right. Commiseration. "You have to pull the engine back out to get at the cam, don't you?" Right. Poor me.

"How'd you manage to get it together wrong?" Bruce still wanted to know.

"Christ, I don't know. I sat there and stared at it for a whole day. I've got diagrams all over the barn wall where I was trying to figure it out. It just melted my brain."

"Yeah," Jimmie said, "it'll do that. One time on the way back from Boston we had a distributor jump out of its slot. Jumped right back in, half a turn out of phase, and we like to never figured out what was wrong. Spent the night in sleeping bags right there beside the road, waiting for enough light to work on it."

"Jumped out and popped right back in again, eh?"

"Yeah."

"Amazing."

"Yeah. Well. Let's go get something to eat."

"Listen," I said, "I really appreciate the help. Even if it didn't work. If you guys need a warm place to work on your trucks this winter, you're welcome to use the barn, any time."

"If you ever get your truck out so there's room," Bruce said.

"Yeah. Well, yes, got to do that first."

"Maybebigfourwheeldrivenexttimepowerful," said Strell, as usual.

They left. I pulled the barn door shut after me. Shit. Well, let's not get hasty and rash now. Just because this stinking sag-ass trash heap happens to have its cam in backwards, let us not lose our patience. Just because the God damned ball-breaking ass-licking rotten scum-bag of a pig fucker is eating me alive, driving me right into the ground from fatigue and drudgery and boredom and hate and despair. Patience.

That's that. At least the bolts are clean and freed up, and taking the truck apart again won't be such painful work. Have to put up the false wall — be colder'n a bitch any day now. Order a new gasket set. Pay a little more attention to labeling stuff as it comes off. Have to trust that goddamn hoist and chain one more time. *Two* more times, engine out, and engine in. Just to bust the engine down far enough to get at the cam, revolve it half a turn, and bolt it up again.

Shit.

Then I thought I would quit and eat some lunch myself, but I decided I might as well put the truck on the stands, to prepare for a serious assault on the engine. And once it was on the stands, I figured what the hell, take a look at those valves, just to confirm my deepest suspicions. So I turned the crankshaft to the top-dead-center mark, turned it over 180 degrees, then started it into the second 180 degrees of crankshaft revolution. Checked Ray's instructions, then checked the valves. The exhaust for number one was opening. That was correct. Checked number six: intake was opening. Also correct. It didn't make sense. The cam was okay.

I remembered Jimmie's story about the jumping distributor. Was he trying to tell me something? That would sure enough make it difficult to figure out why an engine wouldn't run. What if that happened to start with? During, um, assembly?

What if? Someone had carefully scratched cylinder numbers on the six nipples for the sparkplug wires on the old distributor cap, and I'd just as carefully transferred the numbers to the new one and rechecked the

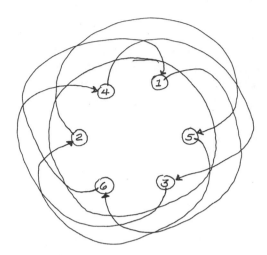

Got it ? Got it .
Don't know why
I ever got confused .

firing order against the book. The cap would only go on one way. But in a previous, rather arcane conversation with my expert friend Sepp, he'd mentioned that it didn't really make any difference which of the six nipples hooked up to cylinder number one, as long as the firing order was correct thereafter from that starting point.

I pulled all six sparkplug wires out of the distributor cap, juggled them for a minute, stared off into space, tried to think — *hard* — plugged them in again one-half revolution from their original location. Moved sparkplug wire number one from two o'clock to eight o'clock on the distributor cap, and so on. Not sure, not sure for a moment, but trickling around the back of my head was what was beginning to feel like a revelation.

Grabbed the jack and slid under the truck to take it off the stands. (*Watch it!*) Set it on its wheels. Carefully wiped my hands on a rag, and then sauntered — oh, cool as a New Hampshire breeze now — around to the cab. Got in. Pumped the accelerator a couple of times to squirt some raw gas. I was assuming that the run down the hill, with the innards finally getting a chance to move around a bit, had loosened things up enough that the starter might be able to do the job. Pulled the choke out halfway. Hit the starter.

Groan. Groan-groan-groan. (Ignition, you dumb shit.) Turned the key. Groan-groan-groan-groan . . .

Vroooom!

Holy shit. It was running.

CHAPTER 20

Zen Trucking

Vroom indeed, it was running away with itself, thanks to by-guess-and-by-gosh carburetor adjustment. I scrambled from the cab, grabbed a screwdriver, and dashed for the hood to get things settled down before the engine melted itself. As I turned the corner at the front fender, I realized that liquid was running out onto the floor, so I reversed myself and hit the ignition switch to shut off the engine.

The liquid seemed to be, yes it was, crankcase oil (but the truck would run), pouring from a plug-hole I'd overlooked — a nicely threaded aperture hidden behind the generator. (But the engine ran.) I cleaned up most of the mess, found the missing plug in my collection of mysterious leftover engine parts, inserted it. (And the cam was not in backwards.) Checking the oil I found that in those few seconds of running the engine had dumped almost its entire five quarts of oil onto the floor, which was at least some indication that the oil pump worked okay. (So did the engine, don't forget that, the engine ran. The cam wasn't in backwards and I didn't have to pull the engine out again, and I could hit the starter and it would start right up. Just like a real truck.) I replaced the oil, and rigged up a booster throttle-return spring, which would help forestall the engine's tendency to run away with itself before I could get at it.

Groan, etc.; it started right up again. The plan was to drive it immediately out of the barn (thus avoiding carbon monoxide poisoning) and get it idled down, running sweet, outdoors. I pulled it into first gear; it wouldn't go. Tried reverse; zero. Pushed it up into second, released the clutch, and it managed to lug on out of the barn, moving itself under its own power. (Look here, a flipping miracle, this truck I built is running.) I jumped out to get the engine idling properly and shit, more liquid spewing, shut it down again. *Another* missing plug, this time hidden behind the starter, and a trail of crankcase contents from the parking spot in the barn all the way out the driveway. This could go on all winter.

But I had a running truck. I floated into the house to regroup around a peanut butter sandwich. Euphoria began setting in. I did it. I figured the son of a bitch out.

During round two, I removed the starter motor, replaced the last oil plug, replaced the starter, refilled the engine with the oil I had left (which was stiff, heavy, old-fashioned single viscosity thirty-weight), failed to restart the engine with the cold and the heavy oil, and pushed the truck by hand back into the barn for the night. In round three I replaced the heavy oil with lightweight break-in oil, recharged the battery, drove the truck around the loop and discovered that indeed I did not have first or reverse gears and that the right rear brake would have to be rebuilt. In round four I rebuilt the brake, rebled the brake system of air bubbles for maybe the ninth time, readjusted the shift linkage to get first and reverse gears and lost second and third in the process; re-readjusted the linkage so it worked, and discovered that the exhaust system, which I'd tried to cobble out of old pipe and leaky muffler, was falling off. In round five I found more coolant leaks and discovered that the battery was not charging.

But I had a running truck.

I had a highly illegal running truck, with no truck bed on the back and thus no taillights, holes in the floorboards, cracked door glass, and not enough traction — for lack of weight on the rear wheels — to pull itself out of a medium-sized mud puddle. But the steering sorted itself out, the brakes came around, the engine settled down and began ticking over like the *Queen Mary*. The clutch felt stout. It was going to work out. What's more, with all that cleaning and painting, unrusted bolts and the removal of years-long accumulations of grease, it was possible to diagnose troubles, find the leaks, *fix* things.

Originally — secretly — I had envisioned a perfect shakedown cruise. Six hundred miles to the south there is a farm inhabited by loved ones. I understand it is littered with broken trucks, some of them Dodges. The reports I receive are garbled, but evidently, although they get some use out of these trucks, none of them is, you know, *right*. Not strong and dependable. They keep complaining about their trucks.

I could fix them. Stowing my tools in *The Harry S. Truman* I would cruise south to Downhill Farm, coping with the last minor idiosyncracies of my truck on the way. I would arrive, the visiting pro in now-perfect truck, to restore order and virtue to their lives and their busted Dodges. Provide real-world coping power for these dizzy poets, who scatter good trucks over the hillsides like discarded beer cans. *Teach* them about the necessities of metal, lubrication, and lock washers.

My first shakedown cruise was the half-mile loop in front of my house, and I barely coaxed the truck home, boiling and spewing. My second shakedown cruise was a repeat of the first, and those two half-mile trips together occasioned five days of adjustment and repair. My third such trip was a little longer, and I began to realize that shaking down my truck would be a process of minutely widening concentric circles, usually ended by a dash for the barn to avoid a tow home. Meanwhile, at Downhill Farm, they seem to work with their busted trucks. I work *on* my whole one.

The dream rescue mission was no sillier than my dream truck had been, the Platonic Ideal of truckness: that scenario in which I would fix everything, make everything perfect, put it all back together perfectly, and thereafter drive and enjoy my perfect truck.

I did not end up with a perfect truck. The passenger-side door opens altogether too easily, the one on the driver's side only by brute force. The entire cab permanently tilts slightly forward, settling down over rust damage to the forward door posts, a solution for which so far escapes my ingenuity. The truck doesn't start too well in the cold — despite a block heater — without a hot, fresh charge on the overworked battery. (We've forgotten, in this twelve-volt era, what a tenuous and thready kind of cranking power we used to depend on to start our six-volt vehicles.) The heater feels like a mouse breathing on my foot. The fuel gauge still doesn't work. The truck doesn't meet any government standard for safety or pollution control — the idea of a propane conversion seems a little silly, now, in view of the truck that it is. So I don't know how long I'll be allowed to drive it on the road. If I can keep it running.

In other words, for all my foresight and mechanical rectitude, I am back there with my freak friends, nervously tricking and conniving my truck along between disasters and breakdowns. Automotive security — the seductive dream of technological armor against the whimsies of nut, bolt, adjustment, rust, dumb iron — proves every bit as elusive as the other kind of security. And, very likely, every bit as enslaving. Ned's pail factory in motion.

I am supposed to be able to say, at this point, that I love my truck. Well

. . . not quite like that. Love it and hate it, a love/hate relationship perhaps. Love it when it starts and goes, hate it when it makes me work on it in the cold. I guess I love it when my head is right. If it has a recognizable character, it is its willowy softness, sighing and groaning as it moves, absorbing the road's vicissitudes. Its tired old structure has sagged and relaxed. If I get into the truck with my head back in workshop-manual mechanicalness, then this softness is offensive. The truck seems a failure.

But if I turn my head around, if *I* can sag and relax — if I judge the truck not in .003s of an inch but in the throb I feel under my left foot that tells me yes, the clutch is holding, it's going to work, the truck will go now — then I can love it. Until the next time it breaks. Roof don't leak when there ain't no rain.

Epilogue

So, MAYBE none of it worked out. Not project, process, or product, not gesture, philosophical statement, or symbolic act. Technology neither banished nor embraced, and myself, for all that attitudinizing on the subject, as hung-up as ever. Time, money, effort, and pain invested, and by golly sure enough I did not find God out there in the barn. Nor emerge anointed as King Engineer, the certified-public-adult-grown-up handyman. In fact I emerged with a semiwrecked and grease-spattered barn, two dozen coffee cans full of nuts and bolts, and a beat-to-shit old pickup truck. A little beat-to-shit myself in the process.

Or maybe it did work: it's just a truck. Finally, by God, it is just that. Got it running in late November, put on the rest of its parts, made it legal. Hauled five or ten loads of accumulated crap to the dump, started making it work. As much last-minute truck work as we could devise, at the tag end of the year. Then, heavy snows and a six-volt starter — and no real need of the truck in the damped-down, low-metabolism months of deep winter — and it was only sensible to give it some respite. Park it out of reach of the snowplows and the road salt, winterize it thoroughly, put it by. Plenty for it to do when the winter is over.

The first part of this obsession was to start searching for the truck precisely on the vernal equinox: missed appointment number one of an endless string of overblown symbolic acts that I never did get around to. But on December 21, the shortest day of the year, when even the dimmest and most primitive of the warm-blooded creatures had long since packed it in for the winter, I put the truck to bed. Pulled it up snug beside the barn, blocked the tires off the ground, carried the battery into the house. Gave the upper cylinders a squirt of oil, stuffed rags into the more gaping body holes. Sleep tight. Then I collected tools in the barn for a while, coiling extension cords, dumping stove ashes, gathering the cans of scattered off-size remnants of the truck's unwanted nuts and bolts. The workshop was about to shuffle itself into a reasonable order when I tripped over a berry basket containing 17,834 old roofing nails, strewing them the length of the barn. Fuckit, I said, bolting the barn door.

Enough. I had gotten over my truck. Oh, I'd get it going again in the spring when we needed it, but for now, the hell with it. No more chafed and bleeding hands, no more eyes full of penetrating oil. No more knots of muscle in the middle of the back from stoop-work over accumulated road grime and rust. No more lying on my back in the semidark, reaching up into cold grease and rusty razor blades to work a bolt loose. Or put it back on. No more of that madness. Fuck Process.

Christmas coming. Time for our annual argument. Do we take one of our own trees, which admittedly need thinning but which we hate to cut? Do we buy a commercial tree-farm Christmas tree, which we also hate to see cut but which was grown for that purpose, is already severed from the earth, and will only be thrown away if someone doesn't buy it and enjoy it? Thus encouraging the hypocritical rip-off artists who merchandise the bleeding things? Or hey, I've got it, why don't we adapt holiday and ceremony to surroundings. Why don't we really get in the spirit of living in northern New Hampshire, and instead of having a Christmas tree, why don't we have a Christmas rock? Haul in a chunk of native granite, stand it in the corner, hang lights and candy canes on it, the whole thing.

Another one of my ideas that will never sell.

So we'll have a Christmas tree, and friends will be here, and good food, warm fires, drinkin' and smokin' and laughin', a nice time. Your basic traditional cheery. Then bank the fires, snuggle in for the long pull, wait it out. Endless winter. January, February, March, April. Most of May. Creek will eventually thaw. Will eventually warm up enough to permit the intrepid skinny dipper. Green will return. Woods smells and wildlife will reappear. Dogs and cats will go berserk, leaves come back, birds again. The whole aching, fecund, messy, glorious time. Marvelous.

Next year's garden should be a natural wonder. Hell of a lot to do. Hay mulch, fertilizer, fence posts and wire to haul, all the dead crap to remove from the garden plot, and the horseshit to put in. Thank God we've finally got a truck.

If I can get it started. I may need some help with that. It's funny — I got into that whole mess in the first place out of some sly, ego-trippy impulse to try to teach a rude object lesson about the mechanical irresponsibility of my freak friends. Show them how they ought to be doing it. How come I always have to ask them to help me make my truck work?

Not to worry about the spring, anyway. Plenty of trucks around. We all have these trucks, see, and someone'll be able to get one going. I see that now. It wasn't clear before. I thought I would rebuild a truck, and then have a truck.

I thought a truck was something that either works or needs fixing. Wrong. A truck works and needs fixing. Separating work with truck from work on truck is indulging in spurious dualities. Workshop-manual thinking. I'm going to have to learn to cut that out.